REDEEMED AMBITION

Balancing the Drive to Succeed in Your Work

RALPH T. MATTSON

REDEEMED AMBITION

Balancing the Drive to Succeed in Your Work

RALPH T. MATTSON

MOODY PRESS

CHICAGO

Scripture quotations marked (NEB) are taken from *The New English Bible with the Apocrypha.* New York: Oxford University Press, © 1961, 1970 The Delegates of the Oxford University Press and The Syndics of the Cambridge University Press. Used by permission.

Scripture quotations marked (NIV) area taken from the *Holy Bible: New International Version®.* NIV®. Copyright © 1973, 1978, 1984 by International Bible Society. Used by permission of Zondervan Publishing House. All rights reserved.

Scripture quotations marked (NASB) are taken from the *New American Standard Bible,* © 1960, 1962, 1963, 1968, 1971, 1972, 1973, 1975, and 1977 by The Lockman Foundation. Used by permission.

Scripture quotations marked (RSV) are taken from the *Revised Standard Version* © 1946, 1952, 1971 by Division of Christian Education of the National Council of Churches of Christ in the United States of America, and are used by permission.

Scripture quotations marked (KJV) are taken from the King James Version.

The use of selected references from various versions of the Bible in this publication does not necessarily imply publisher endorsement of the versions in their entirety.

ISBN: 0-8024-7919-7

1 3 5 7 9 10 8 6 4 2

Printed in the United States of America

To

Conor Garrett Mattson

CONTENTS

KISSING A FROG

smashingly pretty young woman once kissed a frog. It appeared that all she was doing, beside closing her eyes so she could not see what she was doing, was reacting in compassionate response to a reptile's pitiful request. It turns out, however, that she either was amazingly prescient or she suspected that something special must be happening, given the fact she was conversing with a frog.

Whatever, as her pursed lips made contact with the fixed, bony smile of the frog, an extraordinary transformation took place. The lime green frog exploded into a handsome, tanned young man who not only looked like a prince, but was one. This eruption was a spectacular and satisfying surprise to the young woman and certainly a matter of enormous relief to the prince.

The prince was clearly an intelligent man with high aesthetic tastes. We know this to be true because he immediately proposed marriage to the extremely charitable young lady who had saved him from his strange reptilian imprisonment.

If you don't already know who got him into this strange predicament, you will need to go back to the fairy tale from which this plot comes. My reference to the story is merely to introduce the horror of being turned into what you are not, and the sheer delight of being set free from such a condition—especially if beauty itself is the agency of such freedom. Like the prince, most of us want to be someone and to accomplish something, and it has nothing to do with sitting on lily pads, whatever form such an existence may assume in each of our lives.

We can imagine the despair of the prince prior to the kiss as he contemplated the possibility of remaining a frog the rest of his life. He knew he was meant for more than that, even if he happened to be confused about what a prince actually does beside waiting to be a king. This probably was so strong an idea in his heart that the possibility some egret might come along and snatch him for lunch didn't look so bad if he would never be free to attain what he desired.

Certainly, as a frog, the prince had a single-minded ambition. It was not to be a frog, but to be himself. Once he was back in his own skin, his ambition changed to marrying the beautiful woman who saved him from an amphibious future. I am sure that once married, his ambitions refocused upon other goals, and then still others, each new goal bringing him further along in his princely life. Similarly, we too go from one ambitious hope to another, or in the case of rigorous achievers, from one ambitious goal to another.

Whether our ambitions are confused or planful, in the end we want our lives to count for something, to be important, to have some overriding value, to be ultimately satisfying. Such hopes reside in the young and old, the high achievers as well as those who are struggling to find a path. It is true of the financially secure as well as those who repeatedly flirt with bankruptcy. It is true of reprobates and the spiritually ignorant as well as those whose primary goal in life is to discover and follow God's will.

Perhaps the words used to express these concerns are concrete, words such as *fame, security, career, success,* or *wealth.* Perhaps they are philosophical or theological terms: *destiny, meaning, fulfillment, calling,* or *purpose.* Either way, sometimes the words seem completely banal, incapable of articulating the depth of our longings. We move ahead in life prompted by some kind of ambition to become the someone we either hope to be or we think we ought to be, often confused about who that is.

Popular Christianity's response to the confusion is to merely present Jesus Christ as the answer to this and every question of life. There it stops. This response is too facile a generalization to translate into the stuff of living out a day, much less a life. However, the Jesus disclosed by the Scriptures is another matter. The biblical perspective provides the most astounding vista of human destiny to be found. It is from this vantage point that the following chapters have been written.

Though contemporary life is far more complex than any of the biblical writers could have imagined, the profound truths they engaged retain their power. They infuse joy into some of our most mundane moments. They can guide our decisions as we ascertain the meaning of work and decide what paths to take. Aided by them, I presume to take up the topic of your ambition and what to do with it.

As a Christian, I build my thinking from a base of optimism. However, genuine Christian optimism is realistic. While we naturally appreciate the joy of attaining success, we cannot deal with the subject of ambition without recognizing that sometimes we end up in situations, relationships, and roles we don't want. Worse, too often we may be powerless to change the conditions that brought those situations about.

Think of the prince's predicament if no woman, beautiful or plain, could possibly even think about stooping to kiss a frog. You would then get a hint of what it means to be in a permanent place in life that doesn't fit and will never fit. Nevertheless, optimism will reign, as we will see, for very good reasons.

PART ONE
THE SPECTACLE OF AMBITION

As he was valiant, I honour him, but as he was ambitious I slew him.

Brutus in *Julius Caesar*
William Shakespeare

Keep away from people who try to belittle your ambitions.
Mark Twain

CHAPTER ONE

OH, TO BE DISCOVERED!

To prod our imaginations with a frog and a beautiful young lady seems appropriate for our subject. After all, our preoccupation with ambition involves imagination as well as rationality. Movies, television, and books have bolstered our daydreams with the furnishings of an embarrassingly familiar plot. Though decked out in a variety of settings and costumes, the theme remains the same, always centering around the discovery and appreciation of our particular genius.

Sometimes children fantasize about leaving home when they feel they are being ignored by their parents, but they do so with the certainty that they will be enthusiastically rediscovered. They imagine aggressive pursuit and large-scale repentance on the part of Mom and Dad. Adults don't stray far from the same idea.

Stranded on an island surrounded by vast seas, the shipwrecked survivor wonders if he will ever be found. Have all his family forgotten him? Are no friends searching for him? The island is far from the lanes usually traversed by ships. Perhaps he will never be found and will spend all his days alone.

Days go by with emotions ebbing and flowing between hope and dejection. But one morning a passing vessel is sighted as a dim silhouette on the horizon. With exuberant shouts no one else can hear, our hero rushes to the island's pinnacle where he has stacked a large pile of wood in the hope that some day he would need a signal-fire. Hurriedly the match is struck, the tinder ignited. Hope soars with the increasing height of the flames and then gives way to shouts of delight as the ship makes a slow turn toward the island. His signal has been seen. What excitement courses through him as he whoops, shouts, and dances in anticipation of discovery!

Whether we live surrounded by a sea of strangers in a city or are stranded in a small town, we dream of discovery. We long for our destiny to come bearing down on us, like that ship steaming toward the island with its bonfire signal. We see people crowded at the railings of the ship trying to get a glimpse of us, and we anticipate the delight of the rescuers leaping out of the launch to greet us. We bask in the focus of their excited questions. We glow with self-importance as the rescuers begin to realize that they have done more than aid some marooned unfortunate. We can tell they are thinking, "Here is a gem, someone of great worth. A treasure has been discovered."

The recurring Broadway and Hollywood versions of this hackneyed story replace the shipwrecked survivor with what has now become a myth of the struggling actor, dancer, or singer who finally gets a break. The essential scene is a standing ovation for the new star. Bows. Bouquets. More bowing. Cheering crowds who won't leave. How many thousands of people have repeatedly projected themselves onto those stages or their equivalents?

There is the morose high school soccer player, who has barely missed being cut from the team, slouched on the bench during a game. He stares into space as he imagines the coach stunned by the sudden loss of his star player through injury. The coach is forced to look at what he has on the bench. Reluctantly, he gives a nod of his head, and suddenly our high schooler is in the thick of the game. It doesn't take long before the play moves toward him and then includes him. Swiftly he realizes how to make an unbelievable move. With a tied score and seconds to go, he seizes control of the ball and gets a goal. Before the wild, roaring crowd can get on its feet, a new soccer star is born.

Then there is the college student whose merely adequate looks are so transformed by imagination that a rather noisy party becomes quiet as he or she makes an entrance. The silence causes the most popular and most striking-looking person on campus to look up, eyes widen in astonishment and . . . another discovery!

True, this is the stuff of trite movies, romance paperbacks, commercials, and soap operas. But equally true is that these are also the plots in millions of imaginations. The person who has not engaged in similar daydreams at one time or other is probably rare indeed. Yes, the more intellectual person might frown upon a preoccupation with athletics or physical appearance. Instead he might imagine a packed lecture hall, with an audience hushed by the mental gymnastics of a world-renowned physicist. The physicist is suddenly astonished by someone's objection to a conclusion derived from the lengthy equation written on the board. Needless to say, the physicist is forced to recognize a new genius as the gaping, astonished audience turns to see the source of the audacious challenge—backed, of course, by an unbelievably brilliant, clearly articulated analysis.

Almost everyone admits to some version or other of the above. It is a universal phenomenon.

- "Washington is on the phone, sir; the White House."
- "Where did you learn to play the guitar like that?"
- "Who belongs to that extraordinary voice?"
- "But—how did you get past the radar barrier?"

Except for a few self-deluded individuals, this penchant for daydreaming oneself into fame and recognition seems harmless. Few people appear to take it too seriously. The realities of life prevent it. A look at the actual soccer score—or into a mirror or at the physics grade or at our surroundings—and sobering reality quickly engulfs us. But what is curious about all of this is that behind all these superficial fantasies is a striking, and not so superficial, fact. Whether we possess outstanding gifts or what we perceive to be average abilities, almost all of us at one time or other are gripped by an assumption that we *ought* to be discovered. Everybody ought to know our name. The world should take us off our island of insignificance. Somehow, though other parts of your mind may argue otherwise, something in us feels that, to be honest, we really *deserve* to be successful and famous, whether or not we achieve it.

All those sermons in church about the value of humility never quite silences this conclusion. Nor are we sufficiently intimidated by night views of the star-spangled heavens, with their galaxies, black holes, and incomprehensible dimensions, which are supposed to put us into our place of insignificance. Astronomical measurements are sobering, but they have no lasting diminishing effect on our desire to achieve goals that are important to us, even if our life appears to be dwarfed by the glory of the stars. Even those who believe humans are merely biochemical processes that totally cease in death hold on to a pitiful hope that they will gain some kind of immortality in the collective memory of mankind through their achievements. "Remember me," they cry. "Remember me."

REALITY REARS ITS UGLY HEAD

There is something odd about this hankering for fame, or for at least some recognition, especially when it is clear that the world is reluctant to pay any attention to our desires. In fact, the world intends the reverse. It is focused on what we can do for it, rather than the other way around. The world expects us to conform to its requirements. We are coerced into spending much of our lives being what others need us to be, expect us to be, or even direct us to be. Our parents began the process and then our teachers took over, only to be replaced in the world of work by managers, bosses, and supervisors.

When we turn away from the outside world and look to our friends for relief, we often find that they too need us to be somebody for them. Except for a few rare souls, often our friends' interest in us is likely to be attached to our response to them, satisfying them, paying attention to them, affirming their values and their ideas, producing what they need or becoming what they intend.

For some of us, these expectations are so frequent that we can be confused in our attempts to define and understand who we actually are behind all those countenances we obediently produce for others on demand. This is not the extreme contrast of a Dr. Jekyll and Mr. Hyde. It is bewilderment produced by the chameleon-like changes required when we move from one role to another as friend, spouse, worker, parent, professional, student, athlete, helper, leader, son or daughter, church member, homemaker, bread-winner, lover, and citizen. In each case we are required to deliver something different. Where is the assurance of who we actually are in all of this?

BENT THINGS

When people fail to recognize the paragons we are, we may acquire things to dramatize ourselves. Cars, clothes, and buildings, which by nature have other functions, can be bent to this need. Linus's hold on his blanket in the "Peanuts" comic strip is only slightly compulsive compared to many a person's grip on a steering wheel. The transporting function of a car very often takes second place to that of proclaiming the importance and value of its owner. This can lead car designers to appeal primarily to vanity, thereby producing an object of questionable design integrity. This attitude permeates the marketplace, inducing us to participate in what is destructive to our values. The more we assume that certain possessions can add value to people, the less we are able to know the genuine value of people, to say nothing of our own significance.

This is not intended to diminish appreciation for quality products nor the fact that the kinds of clothes, houses, furniture, and equipment we select can be legitimate and necessary expressions of our values and personalities. But when we behave as if we acquire value and importance by driving one kind of automobile rather than another, or by living at preferred addresses or by wearing designer clothes, then we have embraced the ludicrous. The millions of dollars made in our economy based on vanity sales are clear evidence of our desperation for some kind of status, even if it is an illusion. There is something within us that demands recognition or importance, and we are willing to pay high prices for it.

Our careers and jobs may be similarly exploited. We may allow ourselves to respond like chunks of clay to the demands of whatever is necessary to succeed in careers our society deems prestigious. Sometimes we scramble over others to achieve career goals that have little to do with the gifts we know God has already built into our frame. Yes, we are innately ambitious for outstanding accomplishments, status, and importance, whether as a big frog in a small pond or as the prince of an extensive domain, be it professional, business, political, or ecclesiastic. From the earnest Christian pursuing God's will to the adolescent fantasizing himself into a rock star, whatever the motive, it is obvious that ambition and the desire for recognized importance drives the plans and dreams of humanity.

CHAPTER TWO

A MIXED REPUTATION

As powerful a human characteristic as ambition turns out to be, it is not universally clear how we are supposed to feel about it. Ambition surely has a mixed reputation. In Shakespeare's play *Julius Caesar*, Brutus summed up what he was convinced was a flaw in the character of the highest leader of the empire. He accused Caesar of being "too ambitious," a judgment he thought serious enough to back up with fatal thrusts of a knife. All the drama of the play spins around that judgment and its consequences.

With condemnation similar to that of Brutus, but hopefully tempered with mercy, many a preacher has called the faithful to place their ambitions on the altar of sacrifice. There our ambitious nature is to be consumed and our lives placed under God's control. Between Brutus and the preacher, it is clear that none of this speaks well for ambition.

On the other hand, many a parent has urged his offspring to stir up ambition. This usually happens in the context of academic studies or potential employment. "Stop staring at that television set and get out and get a job. When are you going to show some ambition and do something with your life?" "If you don't start working

and get your grades up, you are not going to make it in this world."
Parents and teachers are clearly on the side of ambition.

Family and faculty made this clear to me early in my life as a
student. I remember in elementary school receiving official recognition for my academic efforts in the form of a certificate. I can still
recall the graphics of that document. They were impressive to my
young eyes. Greek columns were pictured holding up the temple of
life. Each column represented the virtues of the scholar, and one of
those columns was labeled "Ambition." It was clear to me that it
was considered a virtue right up there with Honesty and Perseverance and Truth. That represented an attitude not too far from the
mind-set of the apostle Paul, who urged us to seek the "higher
gifts," to run races, win the laurel, and gain the prize.

Brutus and the preacher against Mom, Dad, the apostle Paul,
and the whole educational system of America. A mixed reputation
indeed.

CLARITY

Resolving these opposing views requires that we back away
from talking about ambition as a matter of merit or demerit and see
it first as a deep-seated and pervasive characteristic of human personality. Like all human characteristics, it has the potential for good
or ill. From this perspective we can perceive the good of ambition
but then go on to realize how easily such a good can be distorted if
not entirely corrupted. It can bring a person to the pinnacle of
excellence or to the extremity of viciousness. There is an abyss between Mother Teresa and Adolf Hitler, but they both can be characterized as driven by ambition.

Imagine placing Hitler and Mother Teresa in the same category!
Suddenly, something remarkable can happen here. The subject of
ambition can be transformed from a self-centered discussion about
success and fame to the perception of a great stage upon which
each of us acts out his part in the drama of good and evil. Then it no
longer is the inconsequential matter of whether we are sockeroo
sensations in life, but rather a matter of moral quality and eternal
destiny.

On one hand we see the relentless ministry of Mother Teresa
bringing comfort to the abused and dying castaways of India, imparting great value to each untouchable. On the other hand, we see

Hitler's machine guns, gas chambers, and smoking ovens imposing untold horrors upon vast numbers of men, women, and children who were accounted less than cattle.

Good or bad, ambition involves the driving intention to achieve certain goals, to gain particular ends, whether we think in terms of careers or of life itself. From God's vantage point, it is the power that forces us to act upon life's stage and become children and agents of the kingdom of darkness or the kingdom of light. It is the human contribution to a marvelous but persistent process of change that God has woven into the very nature of the universe.

Each of us is moving toward his or her destiny as creation is moving toward a grand culmination, when all the efforts of nature and the process of time itself will inevitably bring us into the dimensions of eternity. We can feel the power of this conatus on levels all about us as birds migrate, grain is planted and harvested, caterpillars transform into flying beauties, history moves us from epoch to epoch, nations rise and fall, and times and seasons come and go. What happens *on* earth is also happening *to* earth. Astronomers describe our part of the universe as moving irresistibly and continuingly toward an unknown, mysterious, gravitational source. What and where is this place to which we are being drawn?

ORDAINED OR CHOSEN DESTINIES?

The processes of nature follow the appointed times of God without thought or choice. Vast stretches of galaxies continue on their preordained paths through space, with no inherent capacity to change directions. The planets rotate and revolve according to the patterns set for them at the beginning of time. Winter snowstorms arrive without a notion to prompt them. The trees flower and give fruit without any decisions.

However, little fragments of willfulness appear. The giant causal process of the universe contains a parenthesis within which curious incidents appear without explanation. Particles do unpredictable things. Animals choose to go there rather than come here and decide to eat this rather than that.

In mankind, the parenthesis is stretched to a grand degree. The incomprehensible space of the universe outside mankind is surpassed by the incomprehensible complexity of willfulness within mankind. Men and women make decisions that not only modify and improve their existence through progress and civilization, but they affect their own destiny. They are empowered to change their own futures, not only in time, but in terms of their destiny beyond time into eternity.

Each of us can decide to follow a narrow path that leads to a future state of sublime realities, or we can take a wide road that Jesus Christ said leads to destruction. Ambition is the driving force of either alternative. Individuals make their way through a complexity of relationships, careers, jobs, and calling to their self-chosen destiny. Within each person there is a power that propels him or her to the desires of his or her own heart. That power is ambition, and it will ultimately get its way and attain the consequences of the particular way we have chosen.

PART TWO

THE GLASSES THROUGH WHICH WE SEE

There are two equally dangerous extremes, to shut reason out, and to let nothing else in.

Blaise Pascal

The third-rate mind is only happy when it is thinking with the majority. The second-rate mind is only happy when it is thinking with the minority. The first-rate is only happy when it is thinking.

A. A. Milne

The fear of the Lord is the beginning of wisdom.

Psalm 111:10 KJV

CHAPTER THREE

HOW CAN WE KNOW?

C onnecting ambition to our eternal destiny seems a far cry from desiring to gain the winning touchdown in a high school football game or being selected as valedictorian. It is one thing to discuss the achievements of our work, sports, and hobbies and the desire for success and another to tie all of those activities to the grandeur of the universe and our eternal destiny.

Some readers might think we are taking things too far. After all, most of us deal with apparently less significant lives than Hitler or Mother Teresa. But even when people think this way, there is something within them that realizes that racing toward the finish line or achieving a personal goal is not a mild consideration within them. Whatever the accomplishments any of us are motivated to achieve in the home, at work, or on the athletic field, we become intensely focused, spending extraordinary energy in attaining results we desire. We do not adjust easily to misfit situations, whether they involve homemaking, being a student, or developing a career. We do not treat casually those activities which appeal to us. We do not feel like ourselves when we misguidedly take well-respected roles in which we have no interest.

Many years of working with executives in corporations, professionals in their own businesses, and individuals going through the process of career development or career change have taught me that these matters are profoundly connected to the realization of a meaningful life. The problem is that most people do not know how to make sense of it all. Jobs, careers, calling, community service, mission, vision, parenting, marriage, and play are all too complicated to fully understand given the inadequate tools our society, churches, and schools have provided.

Yet these add up to the total activity of all our days. These are the ingredients of which our lives are made. That being so, it is important that we know the theme of meaning, the golden strand that connects all of it. It is imperative we know what kind of attention these matters deserve.

MAKING SENSE OF IT ALL

If we are confused about who we are and about success and achievement, there are many who are eager to assist us out of our ignorance, usually for a price. Purveyors of success, wealth, and fulfillment techniques compete for our attention on television, in numerous books, in magazines, and in seminars across the nation. More often than not, the only people becoming wealthy are those selling the books and tapes about becoming wealthy. It is a ludicrous circus betraying the desperation people feel as they attempt to make something out of their lives.

Many Christians, who are supposed to know the difference between the valuable and the valueless, are not immune to these sales pitches. If they do not respond to secular appeals they have the option of choosing Christian versions of the same success-circus appearing in some churches and seminars and in Christian media. It only adds to the spectacular confusion.

An antidote to this nonsense is thoughtful involvement with biblical values, but too many Christians want everything boiled down to the four secrets of success, the seven secrets of power, and the six secrets of getting what we want through prayer. They want it fast and they want it simple. But life, especially modern life, is not simple. The universe God made is complex. Being a person is complex. Life requires more than simplistic how-to-do-it techniques presented with a dash of biblical proof texts. The rich, full, and satisfying life God intends for us requires wisdom. Though that wisdom has several sources, it is rooted in the Scriptures and energized by the Holy Spirit.

> The first thing is to acquire wisdom;
> gain understanding though it cost you all you have.
> Do not forsake her, and she will keep you safe;
> love her, and she will guard you;
> cherish her, and she will lift you high;
> if only you embrace her, she will bring you to honour.
> She will set a garland of grace on your head
> and bestow on you a crown of glory.
> (Proverbs 4:7–9 NEB)

This poetic portrayal of wisdom was inspired and crafted to attract the heart and the mind, the duplex within which wisdom lives. Since ambition also dwells in the heart and mind, wisdom is the only means we can use to effectively plumb its mysteries. Otherwise, if we approach our ambitions merely with the intellect, as if ambition can be understood and tapped merely by the exercise of mere common sense, we may fail to detect the compulsive power of our ambitions.

Too many intelligent people display the curse of being driven by a mindless ambition for us to trust the intellect alone. Yes, we should logically define ambition, but we must go beyond definitions to engage the source of power that will enable us to be good stewards of our ambitious nature. We will thereby attain valuable goals, goals that will have positive, eternal consequences.

PUTTING ON THE RIGHT LENSES

Everyone who intends to ascertain the truth about any matter needs first to look at the lenses through which they are viewing the evidence. Being fallen creatures, we cannot trust our intellects as if they somehow were unaffected by Adam and Eve's decisions. Our emotions, bodies, imagination, intellect, and spirit were all condemned and contaminated by the Fall of mankind.

I find that Christians tend to take the Fall seriously in regard to their emotions and their sexual and spiritual natures, but not their intellectual capacity. We constantly find ourselves confidently making judgments as if the intellect by which we make those judgments is a precise, infinitely dependable, and infallible capacity. Too often an unhealthy dose of the Enlightenment leavens our attitudes.

All one has to do to correct this overconfidence is conduct exit interviews after any meeting we have attended and laugh at our expectation that there would be any precise agreement as to what really happened in that meeting, even if everyone came to a unanimous decision. Each participant's perception of what happened is unique. That is why the development of Christian theology cannot be a purely rational process. It requires the Holy Spirit to gain what the intellect cannot do alone.

THREE LENSES

Given a healthy suspicion about the ease with which we are able to ascertain the truth, for our purposes we can examine the subject of ambition using three different lenses. When the picture from each corroborates the others we may end up with wisdom. Although we will describe each lens separately for the sake of clarity, they must inform one another if we are to gain genuine understanding of the subject. The three lenses are:

> The Bible
> Culture
> Individual Design

They will be discussed in the order just given, two chapters for each lens.

CHAPTER FOUR
USING THE BIBLICAL LENS

The understanding we can get from the Bible is not restricted to specially selected saints or those who have a penchant for Bible study or those with theological interests. A rich level of biblical depth is open to all Christians, even though we possess varying levels and different kinds of intelligence and experience. What is required to gain wisdom from the Scriptures is a direct encounter with the Word of God, not only with what others have told us the Bible says.

Although we should never diminish the importance of scholars and teachers in assisting us, we must understand that their contributions should not supplant our own individual encounters with God's written Word. God has used many scholars throughout the respective histories of the Jews and the Christians to supply us with accurate translations of the Old and New Testaments from ancient manuscripts. Many archaeologists, translators, and linguistic specialists have made their contribution to the splendid array of Bible translations with which we are blessed today. Those who believe that the Bible brings together the most precious documents ever penned are indebted to biblical scholars for their discipline and expert work.

However, because of the ministry of the Holy Spirit within the believer, many a Christian with nothing like the educational background of the persons who have translated the Bible has understood more of what those translations mean than some of the persons who made the translations.

The best person I know to illustrate this is my father. He was born in Norway where, at the age of sixteen, he abandoned school to go to sea. For years he sailed from continent to continent, probably working more than his youthful hopes anticipated, but also gaining extensive learning, though not in formal terms.

I imagine that was fine with my father, if he thought about it at all. After all, academic learning was one of the things from which he had successfully escaped. Clearly, though he learned from his experiences, he was not a scholar.

Eventually my father came to the United States, married, and began a family. He also became a Christian. It was a remarkable conversion. It had some of the dramatic elements of the apostle Paul's Damascus Road experience and produced a man permanently enthused by the wonder of God's grace toward him.

A special feature of this enthusiasm was my father's love for the Bible. All of his children, including me, have a lasting picture in our minds of him engrossed in reading the Scriptures. The worldly sailor became a student and practitioner of the Word of God.

The then Norwegian section in Bay Ridge, Brooklyn, New York, where I grew up was adjacent to a Jewish neighborhood. Our backyard joined the backyards of Orthodox Jews. I can still see my father walking up and down the streets of our neighborhood in conversation with the local rabbi, whose long black overcoat and black hat were duplicated in small by his young sons following.

More often than not, my father and the rabbi would be deep into Isaiah's prophecies about the coming Messiah. Though he was far distant from my father in terms of formal learning, the rabbi nevertheless was attracted by the depth and vitality of what my father taught. He was thereby required to take seriously the claims of Jesus as the Messiah.

It is seldom possible for me to read Isaiah 53 without recalling those boyhood memories. I realize that this is more than a matter of nostalgia, though there is that. I am aware that somehow I had been brought into a high view of Scripture by my parents. It was not a view that came by way of indoctrination. It was a view into which I was initiated by the character of parents who illustrated the power of God's Word in their lives.

That triggered the assumption that the Bible had power to make a difference to me. My mind and imagination had become furnished with the rich stories and metaphors of the God who entered the history of mankind. These were the outstanding ideas that nurtured me as a young boy.

My experience and that of my parents is a repetition of a remarkable feature of the Protestant Reformation, apparent also in the history of revivalism and of spiritual renewal generally. Ordinary people have been and still can be captured by the contents of the Bible. The Scandinavian immigrant church in which I was raised was comprised mostly of ordinary working people, yet they lived in the expectation that the Holy Spirit would ignite a common agreement among them about what God was saying in the Bible, and church members assumed that any believer could understand the Bible. Not only could they understand, but most of the Christians I observed were also able to translate what they learned into the stuff of daily living as they related to one another. I discovered in that church body exactly what the apostle Paul described in his writings.

> Divine folly is wiser than the wisdom of man, and divine weakness stronger than man's strength. My brothers, think what sort of people you are, whom God has called. Few of you are men of wisdom, by any human standard; few are powerful or highly born. Yet, to shame the wise, God has chosen what the world counts folly, and to shame what is strong, God has chosen what the world counts weakness. (1 Corinthians 1:25–28 NEB)

These verses should not be taken as a celebration of ignorance or as support for a smug attitude toward those who have attained a higher degree of education than ourselves. Man's wisdom is wisdom and therefore good. Man's strength applied appropriately is also good. The benefits of civilization, which most of us prefer over barbarism, come from the wisdom and strength of mankind.

The point that the apostle Paul is making is that man's wisdom and strength, even when they are good, are not adequate for knowing God. They are not adequate even in Christianized versions. It is of great value to apply the tools of scholarship in order to gain theological understanding. The tools of hermeneutics are also of value in interpreting the Bible. Neither, however, enables us to come into contact with God or the Word of God, since that requires the Spirit of God, who may or may not exploit the tools we have acquired.

> As for me [the apostle Paul], brothers, when I came to you, I declared the attested truth of God without display of fine words or wisdom. . . . The word I spoke, the gospel I proclaimed, did not sway you with subtle arguments; it carried conviction by spiritual power, so that your faith might be built not upon human wisdom, but upon the power of God.

> And yet I do speak words of wisdom to those who are ripe for it, not a wisdom belonging to this passing age, nor to any of its governing powers. . . . I speak God's hidden wisdom, his secret purpose framed from the very beginning to bring us to our full glory. But, in the words of Scripture, 'Things beyond our hearing, things beyond our imagining, all prepared by God for those who love him', these it is that God has revealed to us through the Spirit. (1 Corinthians 2:1–10 NEB)

This is the perspective we need as we consider our place in life and our gifts, careers, and ambitions. The Scriptures connect our lives to a large picture, and a grand one at that. For them to affect how we perceive and work out our lives we need to be aware of and sensitive to the spiritual power to which the apostle Paul refers. That is our primary resource in living out well-shaped and well-directed lives.

The Scripture is thereby able to illuminate our destinies as faithful believers, but it is a resource that is often ignored or mishandled. Too often the Bible is exploited for polemic goals rather than humbly addressed for spiritual nourishment and insight. In some circles it appears as if it is more important to be correct about what Scripture says than to receive what God would convey through it. Even the devotional use of the Bible often is reduced to ripping scriptural fragments out of context for use as little nuggets of encouragement.

KNOWLEDGE AND FREEDOM

Why does the Bible repeatedly make a case for wisdom? Why does the apostle Paul argue that this wisdom is of such importance

that it has been made accessible even to those who have not attained high levels of formal education? He does so because wisdom
is linked not only to the grand pleasure of knowing God but to freedom. The greater the wisdom a person attains, the greater the freedom he thereby gains.

This is how it works. Man is the only earthly creature who possesses language, which enables the expression of wisdom. Language enables him to conceptualize and to conceive of what might
be. It also frees him from the restriction of dealing only with that
which can be apprehended by the senses.

Unlike the animals, humans can leap beyond the immediacy
of place and time and conceive of other places, times, and dimensions. A person can share the conclusions he makes with others
and thereby build community.

Language enables patterns of choices that in turn enable the
building of cities, nations, and civilizations. With language, a person can conceive of that which he has yet to experience and even
that which is beyond anything he has ever experienced. He can
dream about what he can accomplish.

Language enables a person to ascertain and express ambition
and gives him the freedom to achieve his goals. Language gives
man the power to apprehend the right and wrong of behavior. If
there is no language there is no freedom. In fact, the Bible says that
the ambitious project of building the tower of Babel (see Genesis
11) was dependent upon the commonality of a single language.

> The Lord . . . said, 'Here they are, one people with a single language,
> and now they have started to do this; henceforth nothing they have a
> mind to do will be beyond their reach.' (v. 6 NEB)

The story goes on to describe how God confused their language. This failure of communication caused a dispersion of people
all over the earth, thereby heading off the potential for monolithic
evil.

Language imparted the freedom to build the massive tower of
Babel, and it is the key to the freedom to attain creative goals or to
bring about the reverse. Throughout history, destructive and even
self-destructive ends have been achieved through the freedom of
man. This freedom is in many ways similar to that enjoyed by God

Himself, who is free to create the world, not out of necessity, but out of divine liberty. The universe itself is a product of divine language. God is free to speak it into being.

Though man and God are both free, there is a terrible distance between the liberty of man and the liberty of an infinite God. God does not and, in fact, cannot choose to deny Himself. In contrast, man is free to choose to give up his freedom—and most peculiarly, too often he takes that liberty.

This is universally evident in the Fall of the human race and individually evident in the sinner who refuses forgiveness. The truth mankind has always been required to face is that both heaven and hell will be populated by those who exercised their liberty. Human freedom opens us to unimaginable splendors or plunges us into an abyss of bleakness beyond comprehension.

WHO ASKED FOR THIS?

When we see the possibilities of our freedom, it is clear that we are torn between opposing desires. On one hand, we see frightening possibilities. They make us wish we had never gained a freedom so powerful that it can bring about self-destruction. On the other hand, who wants to give up the liberty of being an individual capable of choosing one's own destiny?

The conflict of these alternatives is intolerable. How do we negotiate our way? How do we know what to do? Suppose we make a mistake? The more we think, the more anxious we become, until wisdom announces that we have access to the grace of Jesus Christ to gain what we ought. He has opened the way to the place we desire to go. How do we know this? The Word of God announces it.

I discover too many Christians who are rich storehouses of information about the Bible and theology and yet do not seem to have encountered much of the Word of God. As a result, their confidence in exercising the freedom they have been given to live a meaningful life is blunted. They are not sure what to do, and indeed seem to have made a career of not being sure. This is in contrast to what I observed in my boyhood, where the mark of biblical understanding was evident far more in the quality of one's actions than it was in any kind of catechism.

An encounter with the Word of God translates into what one does; to act without thought is foolish. For our thinking to be straight, it has to be informed by what God thought. We should not separate thinking from action and feeling except as categories we use in communication. We are to engage life by using all the capacities God has woven into our frame in creating us. Though I do not want to underestimate the value of formal schooling, I know these God-given capacities were not acquired through schooling. They are an intrinsic part of how we are made, and we are commanded by Jesus to fully love God using all of them.

> Jesus said unto him, Thou shalt love the Lord thy God with all thine *heart,* and with all thy *soul,* and with all thy *mind.* (Matthew 22:37 KJV; italics added)

As we consider our lives, ambitions, careers, purposes, and destinies we will miss the grand truth of it all if we do not engage all our capabilities in attaining an understanding of what it means to be a person created by God. In my professional life, too many of those I have counseled about their careers or their organizations wanted me to merely tell them what to do, to give them examples to copy and models to imitate. They wanted me to restrict myself to the practical without much thought of what those actions meant.

If I had given them merely what they wanted, they would have attempted to use techniques for which they had no passion or understanding. So used, those techniques would have gradually declined in power or would have become like an empty religious rite that is observed, but which makes little difference.

We are not creatures who should act without wisdom. We are much higher creations. The more we engage the higher capacities of the heart, soul, and mind of which Jesus reminds us, the greater our understanding and the richer our lives. The heart, spirit, and mind may or may not be blessed with the addition of formal education, but every believer must be empowered by God. It is to these multiple capacities of learning and knowing that I want to appeal as we consider what the Bible says about God, our ambitions, and our work.

A REASON FOR THE WARNING

In some ways, it is odd that I feel it necessary to remind us of how to approach the Word of God, something that should be elementary to Christian living. However, I am urged to do so by the reality of what I have encountered as I have traveled about the United States. When I analyze what I have observed, I conclude that one of the reasons large numbers of Christians seem disconnected to any kind of passion about the biblical Word is the tendency to centralize the source of truth in the pastor or teacher.

Coming from a Protestant heritage, I celebrate the fact that each of us has direct access to God. There is no mediator but Jesus. That is a wonderful foundation stone of Protestant theology, but what we believe intellectually is not often a feature of what our congregations are being taught. Although no Protestant pastor I know is attempting to play a priestly role in matters of redemption, church members today are more often than not encouraged to be consumers in matters of biblical truth. Too often, pastors and teachers seem to prefer being the sole sources of wisdom about spiritual matters. They do not encourage their parishioners to think for themselves or experience God for themselves. Because the pastor is sure that Christianity is true, the parishioners believe it is true.

In this scenario, the more convincing the pastor, the more convinced the parishioner. But what happens to the faith of our parishioners if they encounter a pastor who is not convincing? What happens to the necessary encounter of each believer with the primary documents of the faith, if we become dependent upon others' understanding rather than our own? The wisdom to which I have referred cannot come secondhand. It must be taught by the Holy Spirit to the individual. Each of us must wrestle with the truth in order to gain a viable understanding of what our lives are about, what our calling is, and what is the nature of our ambition. Knowing the facts of the Bible and getting solid theology under our belt is important, but clearly not sufficient. Biblical knowledge needs to be inhabited by the power of the Holy Spirit and made functional in venturesome living.

CHAPTER FIVE

WHAT WE SEE THROUGH THE BIBLICAL LENS

T
he first expression of ambition in the Bible is found in the story of Adam and Eve. Their story, because of its unhappy ending, forces us to consider first the negative portrayal the Bible provides of ambition. When God is involved with a negative, however, the redemptive must follow, which is why a positive view of ambition will end this chapter. The two views combined justify our reference in the second chapter to ambition's mixed reputation.

THE NEGATIVE VIEW

ADAM, EVE, AND THE TREE

Our first view of Adam does not provide a vivid picture of ambition, if it provides any evidence at all. The natural unquestioning inclination of Adam to cooperate with God's expectation that he take care of the garden and name the animals does not seem to demonstrate the kind of energy we see later in Adam and Eve's temptation to eat of the Tree of the Knowledge of Good and Evil. However we might view Adam's initial state, it was ambition that caused Adam and Eve to become curious about the forbidden fruit. The Genesis story tells how Eve became intrigued by the quality of the fruit and its potential for wisdom as portrayed by the serpent.

Ambition was born in alternatives. And God provided the alternatives.

> The Lord God made trees spring from the ground, all trees pleasant to look at and good for food; and in the middle of the garden he set the tree of life and the tree of the knowledge of good and evil. (Genesis 2:9 NEB)

Consider this Tree of the Knowledge of Good and Evil. Without ambition, that botanical Lorelei would not have had any more appeal than any other tree that shaded the gardens of God. God imbedded into the nature of our first parents a capacity to respond to the radical possibilities for good or evil. The inordinate exercise of that capacity was Adam and Eve's downfall, and the story relates how they got exactly the results God said they would if they did what they were told not to do. They gained the knowledge of good and evil, not fully realizing, until it was too late, that knowledge is not confined to concepts. Knowledge may begin with an idea, but it requires experience. Adam and Eve, by their own volition, came to know and experience that for which they were not made.

The first couple's decision cost them, and subsequently us, dearly. God said if they were disobedient they would surely die, and they surely did die, as we too will. Every gravestone on earth is a commentary on the result of Adam and Eve's attempt at self-sufficiency. Death, however, affects more than the physical body. It attacks the other capacities of the human personality, adding up to a staggering price tag.

1. *Death of Spiritual Vision.* Adam and Eve lost the ability to perceive and directly engage the spiritual dimensions that were so familiar to them, including conversations with God. As a result, their children become imprisoned in the merely physical. All subsequent generations have questioned whether God ever did communicate with mankind, or whether He can. Many have even questioned whether God Himself exists.

2. *Ignorance of Gifts.* Adam and Eve lost the work for which they were gifted and the marvelous garden that provided a fitting place for such work. They became laborers instead of workers. They were unable to initiate their children into a knowledge of their

own giftedness. In their ignorance they began to impose upon their children roles that were not appropriate for the way God designed them. To this very day, people are confused about that work for which they are designed. Parents are unable to see the unique landscape of gifted capacities in each of their children. Often they violate them.

3. *Death of Purpose.* Adam and Eve lost their purpose. Their reason for being faded in their minds and imaginations until they were left without a picture of destiny and were unsure about the value of living. They had to concentrate on survival.

This loss of a sense of destiny has affected subsequent generations, who have written books, plays, songs, and poems about the emptiness of life. Though surrounded by a world of great beauty, people are often blind to it, preferring to conclude that life is absurd and ugly. Because they cannot perceive the goals for which ambition was made, they make self-interest a substitute. They impose their ambitions on everyone else, even destroying others in the process of bringing about their achievements.

4. *Loss of Value.* Adam and Eve lost knowledge of their individual importance. They no longer could hear the splendid "It is good!" with which God assessed His creation, of which man was the crown jewel. By losing their position of authority over the world, Adam and Eve also lost the knowledge of their own value. As a result, people every day strain to prove their importance and worth by playing one meaningless game after another. Rarely does a day go by without their weighing the evidence for their importance, especially in comparison to others.

5. *Death of Joy.* Adam and Eve lost the joy of being. The radiance of God's love that swept through their bodies, feelings, and emotions suddenly ceased. Barriers had been raised that blocked the exhilaration of that relationship until it was reduced to barely recollected memories of the irretrievable past. Cisterns deep within Adam's and Eve's personhood, once filled with love, were emptied. Those empty cisterns remain in their offspring. Over and over mankind has attempted to fill them with inappropriate loves.

These five consequences have been reenacted in every human life since our first parents left Eden. We find in our ambitions, this very moment, iniquitous possibilities together with the seeds of potential glory. We possess the power to choose and execute what we intend, but eat Eden's "apple" every time we do so. Our decisions are filled with the knowledge of good and evil, which translate into actions righteous or sinful.

THE UNHAPPY VIEW OF GOD

All of the above has warped our vision of God, who once was mankind's ultimate delight. Because our actions are either righteous or sinful, when we think of God we are likely, if not necessarily required, to perceive Him first as the ultimate Judge. This was an unnecessary role in Eden before the Fall, but it is an unavoidable one now.

When Adam opened his eyes and looked at God he saw first His engaging beauty, whereas we who have never seen Eden first perceive God's scrupulous eye upon our motives and actions, judging the good and the evil and separating the sheep from the goats, the gold from the clay, the permanent, which will endure in eternity, from the straw, which will be discarded and burned. While you and I evaluate our actions from the perspective of our egos, God comes to other conclusions about what is actually happening. We measure with one set of scales, God with another. He is looking at what He created us to be. We are preoccupied with what we want to be.

The Old Testament portrays this formidable God again and again through the judges and prophets. We understand too well the story of Belshazzar's feast in chapter 5 of the book of Daniel.

> The vessels of gold and silver from the sanctuary in the house of God at Jerusalem were brought in, and the king and his nobles, his concubines and his courtesans, drank from them. They drank wine and praised the gods of gold and silver, of bronze and iron, and of wood and stone. Suddenly there appeared the fingers of a human hand writing on the plaster of the palace wall opposite the lamp, and the king could see the back of the hand as it wrote. At this the king's mind was filled with dismay and he turned pale, he became limp in every limb and his knees knocked together. (vv. 3–6 NEB)

> 'Here is the interpretation [of the writing which was inscribed]: God has numbered the days of your kingdom and brought it to an end; . . . you have been weighed in the balance and found wanting; . . .

and your kingdom has been divided and given to the Medes and Persians.' (vv. 25–28 NEB)

The New Testament is not without its stories of judgment. One of the most vivid is that of Ananias and Sapphira.

> [The couple] sold a property. With full knowledge of his wife [the husband] kept back part of the purchase-money, and part he brought and laid at the apostles' feet. But Peter said, 'Ananias, how was it that Satan so possessed your mind that you lied to the Holy Spirit, and kept back part of the price of the land? While it remained, did it not remain yours? When it was turned into money, was it not still at your own disposal? What made you think of doing this thing? You have lied not to men but to God.' When Ananias heard these words he dropped dead; and all the others who heard were awestruck. The younger men rose and covered his body, then carried him out and buried him. (Acts 5:1–6 NEB)

The account continues with the appearance of Sapphira, who was also interrogated by Peter, with the same consequences. She was buried beside her husband.

These and many other stories in the Bible portray God as a judge. The objects of His judgments are the statements and actions of man. This is not a happy view, but it is a perspective necessitated and only made possible by the ambitions of Adam and Eve. It places our lives, ambitions, work, and goals in a context that no one finds easy to accept.

Some of us thought we knew what we were supposed to be and avidly pursued our goals and achieved them. Our achievements in place, we began to strut like peacocks in the glory of our accomplishments. We may do our strutting, but too often not without asking, "Is this all there is? If there is more, will it end up in a judgment that will find me wanting?"

THE REDEMPTIVE VIEW

For a number of years I have had a fat goldfish who spends winters in a tank in my office and summers in a small garden pool. Its whole day is occupied with eating. If a baby cricket makes a leap into the pool it immediately becomes food. If a mosquito lays its eggs in the water, the eggs end up in the fish. In the absence of such visitors, my fish, with seemingly unending repetition, sucks mouthfuls of gravel into his mouth and expels tiny explosions of gravel, debris, and sometimes particles of food. The food is quickly swallowed and the search continues. Eating and swimming back and forth occupy all its daylight hours.

I am fascinated by the fish. It is curious to observe an existence confined to such efficient, reduced living. It is also a delight to realize what it means to be a person residing at the opposite end of the motivational scale from my handsome fish.

The fish's status is worth appreciating because, though animals are intensely active in taking care of their basic needs, only humans are prompted by ambition—and ambition presents a universe of discoveries and possibilities. In fact, ambition recedes when an individual is focused solely upon survival. It only begins to operate in full expression when such needs are fulfilled. Ambition drives personal advancement and growth. Those are the possibilities we think about once we have bread on the table and a roof overhead.

Ambition is what tells us that taking care of basic needs is not enough. It prompts us to advance beyond such elementary stages to expand our knowledge. It energizes us to engage the complexities of our families, communities, and companies to work and show who we are and what we can do. It moves us, our communities, and our civilization toward advancement, to higher accomplishments. It is dynamic and prompts us to attain the goals and conditions we want.

ALL AMBITION IS ROOTED IN GOD

Curiously (only because ambition is commonly associated with pride), ambition exists because that is how God designed us.

> God said, 'Let us make man in our image and likeness to rule the fish in the sea, the birds of heaven, the cattle, all wild animals on earth, and all reptiles that crawl upon the earth.' So God created man in his own image; in the image of God he created him; male and female he created them. (Genesis 1:26–27 NEB)

From the very beginning, man was made not merely to be occupied with his own survival, but to enhance the survival of other creatures by ruling over them. Man began with this ambition. If man is ambitious and created in God's image, doesn't that logically require God to be ambitious in some mysterious divine manner?

YES?

One is tempted to answer yes, if by doing so we recognize that the very nature of creation, for which God alone is responsible, is a highly elaborate system of nonstop development and advancement. As a normal condition of life, we are required to move through time from event to event. Even our present moment is never static. It pushes us into the future, which becomes the present just before sliding into the split-second past. That is how we flow through time on a journey that will bring us through death into immortality. All that change and forward motion must have its source in God. Nothing can come into existence on its own.

NO?

We are also tempted to answer no because we know that though we advance through time, God doesn't. God does not live within time, because time is a creature and a creature cannot contain that which created it. God does not advance because there is nothing into which He can move. If He could move ahead, He would discover that He is there already. God cannot advance toward something outside Himself because there is no outside to God. He is unending. There are no possible goals outside Him. In fact such ideas are absurd and are only possible to conceive when we impose a human mode of existence upon God.

CONCLUSION

The fact that God is not in time does not suggest that God is static, since, obviously, He is dynamic. We can tell that simply by the presence of the universe, which required action on the part of God in order to come into existence. We can also tell He is dynamic by the kind of universe He made. It is, in every detail, dynamic from the continuous expansion of space to the cycle of the seasons. Absolutely everything is in motion. There is not a particle of the universe that is still. The chair in which I am now sitting as I keyboard this chapter into my computer is comprised of vast numbers of molecules in constant motion, though I do not see any motion. In fact, the chair feels quite solid and substantial as I sit in it.

My chair is also moving through space, though it appears to be still as I see it in relation to other objects in the room, as is the room in which all the objects have been placed. However, it is an elementary fact that, together with me and my whole environment, the chair is moving swiftly through space as the earth rotates fast enough to bring us from total darkness to the peak of sunlight in twelve hours. That requires us to move through space much faster than a baseball hurtling across a Major League field. Our path through space is made even more complex by the rotation of the earth plus the movement of our galaxy through space. All this dynamism in the universe reflects the personality of the divine Artist who brought it into being.

In the same way we look at the elements of a painting by Paul Cezanne and make statements about his style, so we can look at the universe and say something about the pattern of God's style. Both products, the universe and the paintings, say something about the character of those who created them. The apostle Paul spoke of this.

> His invisible attributes, that is to say his everlasting power and deity, have been visible, ever since the world began, to the eye of reason, in the things he has made. (Romans 1:20 NEB)

The dynamism of the universe is a visible expression of the power of God. In the book of Job, God is rightly described as being "excellent in power" (Job 37:23 KJV). What has this to do with ambition? Ambition triggers the power within us to accomplish results. As we observe the universe, we see God doing in large what we do in small through our work and careers.

This dynamism is a feature of personality. Our work on earth mirrors God's work of creation. All power can only come from God, including that of ambition. The objectives to which the power of human ambition may be applied are not always inspired by God, but its source is God. Even the murderer, whose intent is hateful, carries out his objective using God-given skills and energy.

A CONTRAST

To deepen an appreciation of how the power of our ambition is rooted in God's power, compare the biblical picture to that of Buddhism, which recognizes no God at all. In its different forms,

Buddhism denies the value of material things and the senses. They are to be transcended until they no longer cause any reaction. The concept is expressed as follows:

> Immaterial things are more peaceful than material, cessation is more peaceful than immaterial things. (*Itivuttaka*, p. 62)

Jews and Christians stand against this denial of creation and neither mistakes a fallen world for a bad world or pits the spiritual against the physical, because God made both. Because of His very nature, God could not possibly make a bad world, and He certainly is insistent about saving the fallen one.

God is the inventor of the mind and the spirit and the body, and He made them unified and good; but now they are fallen and fragmented. What is His reaction? He does not deny them even in their fallen state. He redeems them.

My ambition is part of my mind and spirit and body, so it too is fallen. But here again the redemptive power of God is at work to convert that which is centered on itself and set it free to accomplish that which is productive and praiseworthy.

When Brutus condemned ambition in Caesar he was seeing its fallen state. When the apostle Paul prods us to press forward to win the prize he is describing redeemed ambition. Our ambitious nature can be hideous or superbly beautiful, but it was always meant to be the latter. As Christians, we must reject the Buddhist ideal, which denies ambition, and we must also reject any Christianized version of such a perspective. We must look instead to a different process. We expect the sanctification of our ambition rather than the rejection of it.

PROBING DEEPER

Are we, who are designed with an irrepressible intention to accomplish as much as we can in life, a product of happenstance? Could our ambition, with all its potential for trouble, have been designed differently? Were there other options?

I believe it is fruitless for us to think of God weighing such options as we do. We might be able to say that whatever God does is always the best choice without having to say it is the only best choice. But this sort of thinking is linguistic nonsense because we are dealing with the unknowable, requiring the language of eternity rather than the vocabulary of time and space. We can, however, look at the root of ambition as it appears in the Trinity and capture a deeper sense of what the Scriptures mean when they state that we are made in the image of God and why that should make a fundamental difference to our everyday living.

The apostle John states: "All that came to be was alive with his life" (John 1:4 NEB). The universe, people, animals, and music are all dynamic because the God who invented them is dynamic, energetic, active, emphatic, mighty, and powerful. That description is an ingredient of His nature. That is how He is.

But while God is an absolute unity, the "shape" of this unity is expressed in a dynamic trinity of persons. The three interact with one another. The power of love flows from the Father to and from the Son by the Holy Spirit. This flow of love is so intense that the Scripture sums it up with a simple but arresting definition: "God is love" (1 John 4:9 NEB). No wonder that creation itself is described as having been achieved through Jesus, who is the object of the Father's love.

> In him everything in heaven and on earth was created, not only things visible but also the invisible order of thrones, sovereignties, authorities, and powers: the whole universe has been created through him and for him. And he exists before everything, and all things are held together in him. (Colossians 1:16–17 NEB)

The universe, then, is a product of love, and with our appearance in it, an object of love, and subsequently, because of the Fall, the subject of redemptive love. As those famous verses in the gospel of John state:

> God loved the world so much that he gave his only Son, that everyone who has faith in him may not die but have eternal life. It was not to judge the world that God sent his Son into the world, but that through him the world might be saved. (John 3:16–17 NEB)

Now add the following declaration from the first epistle of John, and we must conclude that if we are to fully understand our ambitions we must see them in the context of love.

How great is the love that the Father has shown to us! We were called God's children, and such we are. (1 John 3:1 NEB)

God is motivated by love to act toward us in a way that lifts us into a remarkable and unique relationship with Him. What an act of love that He gives us the power to call ourselves His sons and daughters. What an act of love that Jesus Christ died in order to bring us into such a relationship! The energy of our ambitions need no longer be diverted to prove our worth, since we can accept what God has already declared our value to be.

Without the need to prove our worth, our ambitions have been set free to mimic God's freedom. He set His sights on our salvation "before the foundation of the world" (Ephesians 1:4 KJV; see also Revelation 13:8 KJV) and moved irresistibly toward His goal and achieved it for the sake of love. We, like Him, can now operate in the context of love and set our sights on our goals and achieve that which will delight us, God, and those who benefit from our efforts. We can manage our ambitions instead of being driven by them. We can be good stewards of this precious gift God has given.

That is why there are those who, in the world's opinion, have never risen above anonymity, yet are quite pleased with life even though they are engaged in what many would think are mediocre careers. Are they ignorant and self-deluded? No. If they are required to think about it, they will tell you that they may have not achieved fame, money, or prestige, but they have tried to be good stewards of what God gave them in the circumstances they have been placed. They bask in the pleasure of how God views them.

The good news is that ambition can be exploited to bring about that which is ultimately satisfying regardless of the "high" or "low" context in which it is being exercised. The conclusion is inescapable. Any of us may be pursuing grand schemes or achieving mediocrity with the very real possibility that we cannot differentiate one from the other, but God has opened up the way to know what is worth achieving and has given the power to achieve it.

CHAPTER SIX

THE CULTURAL LENS

I have a friend who, many years ago, regularly flew medical supplies into African villages. Some of the villages were so remote that, before his dramatic arrival, the inhabitants had never seen a white man, much less anything like the mechanical bird in which he arrived. My friend was able to establish a fine relationship with one of the younger leaders of a particular village whose needs required rather frequent visits. One day this leader was offered a ride in my friend's airplane, and without hesitation he welcomed the opportunity.

Though the villager had climbed many a tree, he was not prepared for the wonder of swooping above the forest itself and even above the birds. He was delighted until the airplane climbed high enough for him to see not only his own village, but the next village, separated from his by a long distance. He took one look at both villages, made an exclamation, and went into a moaning fit. His thrashing was severe enough to endanger the frail airplane. It was lightly designed to allow for very short landing strips, and so the pilot had to move swiftly to get his unhappy passenger to the ground. Meanwhile, he could not imagine what had gone wrong.

Safely on the ground, and eventually calmed, the villager made clear that the height had not been frightening. Gradually, repeated questions revealed that what had been so upsetting was the simultaneous sight of two villages, which everyone knows cannot ever be seen at one time. It was not the novelty of the sight that bothered him. It was the impossibility of it. His culture did not conceive of time and space in Western terms. The experience of traveling from one village to another provided his tribal culture with the foundational language of relating the two. But his culture did not equip him to comprehend the visual experience the flight had introduced into his life.

This story is not to suggest that the villager was less intelligent than any Western child just beginning school, who would not have questioned the reasonableness of two villages being seen at the same time. In fact, the story has me wondering, given the difference in cultures, what the village leader perceives about the relationship between the villages that our scientific language cannot contain. What does he know, given his language of thinking, that I cannot possibly know given mine?

SEEING OBJECTS DIFFERENTLY

Language not only includes the verbal, but also other symbol systems and ways of understanding. Medieval Christians, for example, saw objects quite differently than we do. They could not think about functional objects, such as tools, lamps, or bowls, as if they had an existence apart from the spiritual dimension. When they held tools in their hands, they believed each tool's essence reached beyond time and space. That is a perspective quite foreign to most of us.

The medievals lived in a world of comprehensive unity. Innumerable modern Christians live in a dual world where bodies and things are on one side (bad) and the spiritual on the other (good), with both sides at war. This is obviously not a biblical picture, because Jesus Christ is portrayed as redeeming both our spiritual and our physical natures from the bondage of death. It is, however, a commonly held subcultural idea that has limited the thinking and experience of many Christians.

WONDER

The ordinary medieval Christian had a far greater sense of wonder about his faith than almost any of us today are capable of understanding. With that wonder came a splendid array of verbal and visual symbols and allegories to express it. The richness and brilliance of this expression make modern Christians look like primitives by comparison.

The reason we do not have a comparable level of expression for our faith is because our view of the world tends to be perceived more in terms of technical rather than spiritual concepts. Today's Christian can logically deduce from the facts about the world that God created it. The medieval Christian would see the world primarily through the concept of God just as vividly as if he were looking at his surroundings through colored glasses.

None of this is to suggest that we go back to medieval culture. Obviously that is not possible, nor would it be desirable. The point is to provide examples of strong cultural contrasts even when there is common belief. Cultures determine the terms by which we understand things and often determine whether it is possible for us to conceive of certain ideas or even realities. Those terms can expand or limit us.

The experience of thinking is so personal it sometimes has us convinced that our conclusions must be correct merely because we made them. The antidote to such error is to remember that every language is limited, equipping its users to make certain assumptions but incapable of bearing ideas that another language might easily convey. This is not only true of foreign languages in relation to each other, but true within one language as it is applied to prose, poetry, and other literary forms. It is true also of visual, gestural, symbolic, spatial, and sign languages in relation to one another. The aggregate combinations of all these languages make up the expression of a given culture—including that of today's Christian —a matter of high importance if we are to understand anything, including the realities of ambition and success.

When we look at reality through the lens of the Bible and come to a mistaken conclusion, the Holy Spirit or scholars and teachers can assist us in the process of correction. They work from a documented base of truth. When we look at reality through the lens of culture, however, those who would correct us when we need it usually are looking through the same lens as we.

The African village leader, for example, could not have attained a scientific perspective of the two villages from anyone else in his village, since they would all share his cultural assumptions. The only explanation of the village leader's disturbing sight of both villages would have had to have come from outside his culture. There was no language in his village that could interpret his experience.

But he is not alone in that state. That is everyone's fundamental limitation. We not only need other languages but other kinds of languages to grasp certain kinds of knowledge or wisdom that are otherwise beyond us.

CHAPTER SEVEN

SEEING THROUGH THE CULTURAL LENS

oday's Christians are in a predicament similar to that of the village leader mentioned in the last chapter. Our cultural language is inadequate to the breadth of our experience. As a result, we address the subjects of ambition, work, career, and success using the same definitions of those words as the general secular culture does.

While we must know the secular language in order to conduct our lives in the marketplace, we should be making our life-decisions based on a genuinely Christian mind-set. Today, the biblical perspective, which in the past was translated into highly influential, authoritative, Christian cultures, is kept isolated, for the most part, in the academic chambers of our brains. This prevents the Scriptures from informing us in the conduct of our daily lives. They function in our devotions but not in the stuff of our work and careers, where we spend most of our time.

Even those Christian organizations devoted to expanding the influence of the Bible in business, industry, and the lives of executives see scriptural connections mostly in terms of ethics and character. Such matters are important enough to justify their ministries, but they do not make an impact on how business and industry are defined in our society.

Most Christian business people assume the definitions given by the world. Some readers are surprised at the very idea that alternative concepts could exist. Similarly, the church has capitulated to the world even in matters where the genius of the Bible provides extraordinarily powerful perspectives that can and, in my professional experience, do transform how practical organizational matters such as selection, leadership development, team building, and organizational effectiveness are executed.

More than one president, director, and pastor keeps a Bible containing the appropriate principles on his desk but has American Management Association concepts in his head. There is nothing wrong with using AMA concepts when they are true, but for the most part their basic working assumptions about people are the very opposite of what the Bible so wonderfully portrays. No wonder management models change almost annually in corporations. All of this, whether it appears in secular or ecclesiastical situations, displays a strict separation of the spiritual realities from organizational processes, a most unhealthy dualism.

WHAT IS THE EVIDENCE OF THIS SEPARATION?

One feature about the Bible, obvious from the reading of the Old and New Testaments, is that God delights in the great variety of personalities He has created throughout history. He so appreciates human variety that He refers to Himself as the God of Abraham, Isaac, and Jacob—three very different characters.

Yet our Christian culture rewards the diminishment of uniqueness in favor of conformity. Look what would happen in most churches on Sunday morning if an individual were to deviate from the standard dress expected for a Sunday service. There is sure to be a critical reaction, probably not vehement nor audible, but critical nevertheless. One might think that God Himself were being insulted rather than the cultural values of the congregation. This would happen in spite of the fact that God has already given His opinion about the matter in a warning most of us have been raised to ignore.

For instance, two visitors may enter your place of worship, one a well-dressed man with gold rings, and the other a poor man in shabby clothes. Suppose you pay special attention to the well-dressed

man and say to him, 'Please take this seat', while to the poor man
you say, 'You can stand; or you may sit here on the floor by my foot-
stool', do you not see that you are inconsistent and judge by false
standards? (James 2:3–4 NEB)

The expectation of conformity not only involves appearance,
but also the world of ideas. If an individual has a fresh or unusual
way of looking at Christian truth, the reaction from fellow Christians
is not likely to be an open, learning attitude, but suspicion. A creative approach to truth is often interpreted as a flirtation with her-
esy. Meanwhile, points of view that actually do skirt close to error,
but which are couched in familiar Christian clichés and jargon, are
less likely to be questioned. Familiarity and conformity must be
sustained.

As an experiment, go into a Christian bookstore and take up
any current book that you care to, read the first paragraph of any
chapter, and make a guess as to what the remainder of the chapter
will say. Quite often your guess will come close to what the chapter
actually contains. Read a verse presented in a devotional book and
guess what the main point of the devotional will be. You will probably be correct. Listen to the first line of a new contemporary worship chorus and postulate what the next line will be. You need not
ascribe your inevitable accuracy to a display of personal brilliance.

My point is that the same ideas are being churned over and
over until they become our security, our cultural mantra. It all can
be very boring, to say nothing of how the practice positions the idea
of God in the secular mind.

MODELS

What is characteristic in all of this is that Christian culture has
been captured by predictable models. There is a stereotypical model
for the Christian father, the Christian mother, the Christian pastor,
and the Christian leader. We know how they are supposed to look,
act, and talk. There is a particular way we are supposed to pray,
conduct devotions, read the Bible, relate to the church, manage our
money, teach our children, and find God's will. Christians do not
want to learn how to become authentic parents; they only want to
become model parents.

The models appear in too many books and seminars and in too much teaching and preaching to be easily ignored. As a result, Christian individuals, families, and organizations are for the most part uncreative. That leaves Christians vulnerable to the imitation of secular culture in areas where there needs to be Christian originality.

The slick worship programs typical of many of our nontraditional churches appear to be far more informed by the techniques of Broadway than the Holy Spirit. How can the numinous inhabit such a well-meaning but unsuitable context? Imitation is dangerous to the church because it prevents mature, exuberant expressions of our faith. It prohibits the growth of fresh ideas, new approaches to problems, creative worship, dynamic education, and, for our purposes, the discovery of fitting life goals.

Christians do enjoy the variety of characters found in the Bible, and they do agree with the idea of individual uniqueness, but, for the most part, they do not think about how this phenomenon should enhance the way their communities operate. Churches are ill-equipped to identify the unique gifts of their people and nurture and appropriately manage them. That not only affects the quality of ministries but is a detriment to development of Christian lifestyles of high quality. It is odd that we who talk about the indwelling Holy Spirit, who is the creative force of the Trinity, display so little originality in our lives and in the operation of our churches and ministries. This is nothing short of peculiar.

The disparity between the creative ingenuity of the God we worship and the products we, His children, produce today is seldom acknowledged, but it is a symptom that signals danger. It explains why almost every new fad in secular popular music is eventually duplicated by the Christian popular music industry. It is the reason why a subject like the reinvention of the corporation, first presented by secular executives, is now being discussed by certain church leaders, who are considering the reinvention of the church. It is why a year or so after all the co-dependency books appeared in the secular bookstores, Christian versions aping the same idea were being sold in Christian bookstores. With just these few random examples, we can justifiably ask: Who is following whom?

There is a huge vacuum in Christian culture where creative ideas and fresh concepts should be percolating, but that vacuum is being filled by vacuous watered-down secular claptrap. This is not something hidden in a corner; it is everywhere. However, because it is a matter of our cultural eyeglasses, we may not see it. As long as all is morally correct, Christian culture allows itself to be captured.

> READER, behold! this monster wild
> Has gobbled up the infant child.
> The infant child is not aware
> He has been eaten by the bear.
> Alfred E. Houseman,
> "Infant Innocence"

HOW CULTURE AFFECTS OUR FUTURE GOALS

Though we cannot immediately change the culture, we can pray for another Great Awakening to renew our churches and, in turn, transform Christian culture. This surely will be a long-term process. For our purposes now, we can protect ourselves as individuals from shallow thinking and superficial lifestyles, especially in working out our careers and work.

To do this, our faith needs to be more than a collection of inadequately understood hopes. Our confidence in our Christian experience must be based on our own encounters with God, not upon the assurances of our Christian cultural stars, be they entertainers or preachers. We need to hear from God personally so we can gain clarity about what our lives mean and what we specifically are to do with them. Otherwise, we might fall victim to a permanent pattern of procrastination, where no definitive action ever takes place. Or we adapt a lifestyle similar to those of our non-Christian friends, just without the immorality. Or we pursue the development of a career in whichever ministries provide us the assurance that total involvement equals a meaningful life. We thereby gain the reassuring Evangelical label *full-time Christian service,* leaving those who serve God in the marketplace wondering precisely how one lives a life of part-time Christian service—especially since we rightly assume that a relationship with God necessarily involves all of our lives, not fragments.

Does it make sense to conclude that we cannot attain the best unless we give up our current careers to work totally in the context of the church or parachurch organizations? While we know many

Christians do fit that context, should it be assumed that all do or should?

Among Catholics the equivalent phrase to *full-time Christian service* is the term *vocation,* which refers to a call into the priesthood. In the New Testament, vocation refers to the call of the gospel, which God extends to all, and the success of which is seen in repentance and in following Jesus Christ, who gives the call. The changes that thereby take place also include the way we do our life's work, regardless of where we do it. The particular way the word *vocation* is used in the Roman Catholic setting, however, is exclusive, whereas The New Testament usage generally portrays a universal call.

To be fair, in both examples the terms used are intended to be a convenient means of identifying those who spend all their working or professional lives as part of a church or ministry effort. That is their simple purpose. However, in practice, both terms have taken on additional meaning within their respective cultures. It is not unusual for those who come under either classification to enjoy the fact that they have been thereby designated as persons in whom God has special interest. I wouldn't argue against this idea unless it also suggests lesser divine interest in computer programmers, plumbers, engineers, and artists, an assumption that would be a profound theological mistake and would distort reality. We do not need more confusion in thinking about ambition and what kind of work actually pleases God.

TAKING ON AN OPTIMISTIC VIEWPOINT

The above picture of contemporary Christian culture is necessarily negative, but understanding it is the first step in developing a positive approach. None of it is intended to support cynicism or an attitude of superiority. There is a big difference between the substance of the church of Jesus Christ and the oddities that at times may encrust it.

The truth is, we are able to hear the message of the Gospel many centuries after it was first proclaimed and hear it with remarkable purity. That alone justifies profound gratitude to whatever churches are faithful to the Gospel message, regardless of what kind of culture accompanies it. We can always find creative and thoughtful Christians with whom we can commune. There are always pockets of innovation or creativity to refresh us.

For those who are alive today, this is the best time. That is because this is the time to which we are called and the only time we have. It is precious and fleeting. We ought to make the most of it. The negatives in our culture cannot prevent us from living generous, fruitful, and joyful lives as we pursue appropriate ambitions. There is no less power available today from God than there ever was to discover the splendid surprises He has for us. As the apostle Paul wrote,

> Behold, now is the accepted time; behold, now is the day of salvation. (2 Corinthians 6:2 KJV)

In this instance we can use Paul's words to envision God saving us this day from confusion about ourselves, our place, and who He has called us to be. In short, it means salvation from whatever might get in the way of our heritage in Christ, as well as salvation from sin. It pictures the immediacy of our experience with God. That is sufficient, not only for optimism, but for joy. We can always put together a fine feast and invite our friends in to enjoy it with us whenever we need buoying up.

WHAT WOULD OPTIMISM HAVE US DO?

If today's culture is not nourishing, where shall we go to feed? The answer is found in those past Christian cultures throughout history whose accomplishments were so splendid their artifacts are treasured and preserved today even by those who do not entirely understand them. It is useful to take a look at history in order to gain some clarity about our own.

The best source for us is, of course, the Bible. There we see that Old and New Testament characters carried on their lives as if there were vast spiritual kingdoms conjoined with the universe of time and space. They assumed that there was constant intercourse between heavenly personalities and mankind.

There are many examples. The Egyptians discovered their first-born children slain by the Death Angel because of their refusal to release the Israelites. Shadrach, Meshach, and Abednego were visited and protected by someone "who looks like a god" when they were thrust into a furnace because of their faith. Peter was led out of prison by an angel he thought was a vision, but was surprised to find was a very real heavenly agent sent to release him. In short, we see Jews and Christians in the Bible who believed that God was behind the interpenetrated realities of the physical and spiritual, of heaven, earth, and hell, driving them toward a conclusion so spectacular that the imagination alone is able to furnish us with pictures of what lies ahead.

In certain periods of human history this realization was vivid and, as a result, inspired great architectural works that combined technical and spiritual significance. The cathedrals of Chartre, Reims, Amiens, and Bourges in France; Durham, Ely, and Salisbury in England; and the humbler Meeting Houses of New England are a few of many brilliant examples. Their spires, rooted as they are in the grounded nave of the church, stretch upward, higher and higher and thinner and thinner, until they disappear into the heavens.

In the cathedral, the spires without and the vast enclosed spaces within necessitated three things. They required venturesome engineering and creative design fused together by passionate belief in God. Whole civilizations were built upon the premise that the entire creation is a multilayered universe in which the spiritual has intercourse with the physical. We who are in time are being captured by an eternal God through His pervasive spirit of love. He is sweeping millions of people upward, higher and higher into the grandeur of eternity. The stage for this action is the history of civilization. The settings for this drama are the villages, towns, and cities throughout the world. This includes you and me working in our corner of the world.

In some periods of history the grandeur of this vision of reality faded. The excitement and drama of the multidimensional understanding eroded, almost to disappear. But through God's grace small embers of spirituality glowed from time to time, enough to prevent the light from being entirely extinguished. Then it would blaze up again and at times even explode under a fresh outpouring of God's Spirit which, in turn, reshaped civilization.

In the history of the United States, for example, the Holy Spirit has brought periods of revival so that churches were renewed. At times the power of these revivals was so intense that they burst out of the churches into the towns to become the Great Awakenings recorded in our history books. These spiritual moves of God affected the marketplace. They changed the way people did business. They changed education and produced Yale University and Harvard University, which originally operated solely out of the Christian experience. They changed the way towns were designed and administered. They changed the way people thought and lived their daily lives.

The evidence is everywhere. The physical reminders of past spiritual riches are seen in books, art, music, and the architecture of towns and cities all over the United States. This is just a portion of what can be directly encountered all over the western world and beyond. Judeo-Christian spirituality has been the foundation for the most brilliant accomplishments of Western civilization. In fact, there would be no such civilization without it.

COUNTERACTION

As Christians, we can take advantage of our extensive roots, draw nourishment from them, and thereby prepare ourselves to counteract the distortions of secular influences. For example, we live in a highly technical age. We are able to engage technology with great confidence and thereby achieve outstanding advances. These advances are wonderful, but we know that technology itself cannot satisfy anyone's desire for a meaningful life. It cannot contribute much to the inner man, since such vitality can only come from the spiritual domain and, in particular, from a relationship with God.

Yet the technological world is so influential that at times we find ourselves reasoning about God and our relationship with Him in quasi-technical terms that fail to stimulate the imagination or motivate our spirits. As a result, the expressive language of our Christian communities is often not equal to the content of the theology in which we believe.

For example, we often respond to upsetting events in our lives with the supposedly comforting conclusion, "But God is in control," as if He were a master engineer standing in front of a cosmological computer controlling all the details of the universe. Curiously, for a term so frequently used by today's Christian, the word *control* is not used in the entire King James Bible, according to *Strong's Exhaustive Concordance of the Bible*. In other translations, the few times the word *control* is used it is, for the most part, restricted to the idea of political control, self-control, and several instances of

God's controlling specific conditions, such as the onslaught of plagues. We do not have a clear picture of God controlling the world, because that is not an adequate description of the tension between God's sovereignty and man's free will. That tension is portrayed in 1 John as follows:

> We know that we are children of God, and that the whole world is under the control of the evil one. (1 John 5:19 NIV)

The popular use of the word *control* by Christians is incapable of expressing the paradox of the spiritual battle in which we are engaged. That paradox is so large in our lives, we can be very troubled if we are not given better ways to think about it.

There are times when the battle does not seem to make any sense. Events take place that do not seem to line up with the biblical promises we have been taught. Some of these events are hurtful to the body, some profoundly painful to our feelings. We become weary or are wounded. In such situations we need a way to understand and express our feelings and thoughts but find little recourse in contemporary words to do so, especially since the modern church, for the most part, has not valued the artists and the poets who, in viable cultures, provide them.

As another example of technical thinking, consider the frequency with which we use the word *plan* in spiritual matters. We teach about the "plan of salvation" or assure people that "God has a plan" for their lives, as if there were a set of blueprints for every believer to use. There are millions of Christians all over the globe eager to carry out "God's plan for their lives," with God apparently playing a curious game of denying them access to precisely that which they are supposed to fulfill. The frequency of Christian usage of the word *plan* is not matched by an appropriate degree of meaning. It is a dry word to be using about God's passionate will.

Of course, the use of the words such as *plan* or *control* in conjunction with God is an attempt to affirm that God is not a divinity who created a chaotic universe in which anything can happen. God is undoubtedly sovereign, but His unique exercise of that authority is to give mankind decisive power even when that permits an individual to choose death rather than life in Christ.

There is order and design to what God does and we can trust Him, but what arid and inadequate language we tend to use to portray the God who is both the author and the object of history. How empty is the idea that God is in control when any one of us faces the death of a friend or relative for whom we have had great love. Are we supposed to take comfort in the idea that God directly engineered those heartrending events? Surely that is not what anyone means when he uses such words at such a time.

Given the linguistic wealth of the Bible and the traditions of the church, surely we can come up with something better. For example, what were the words of Job when he went through tragedy after tragedy? "Though he slay me, yet will I trust in him" (Job 13:15 KJV). Such language embraces the paradoxes that are part of life. They enable us to intuitively understand that which reason cannot grasp: faithfulness in the face of irrational events. It portrays in the spiritual the same anomaly discovered in the universe when scientists perceived that within the grand unity of the physical universe there are degrees of disorder. Such physical "disorder" parallels that of our lives as described in the great book of Ecclesiastes.

> I . . . saw under the sun, that the race is not to the swift, nor the battle to the strong, neither yet bread to the wise, nor yet riches to men of understanding, nor yet favour to men of skill; but time and chance happeneth to them all. (Ecclesiastes 9:11 KJV)

How rich these words are in conveying the not-so-pleasant injustices of life. Something is released within us when we ponder them. What happens when we look at our life goals using the terms *control* or *plan*? If we say God is in control of our careers, does that mean we do not have to make decisions? Do I just drift from event to event assuming that whatever happens is what God intended to happen? Do I not have a responsibility to exert my own will? Does God make me will what I will? Is my life all planned out? Is God in charge of all planning so that He can decide what path I should take, and all I have to do is obediently follow His blueprint? It appears that neither word is very useful in these matters. Nothing is released within us when we ponder them.

GROWING IN LANGUAGE

We can begin to see the justification for emphasizing language, especially in the practical context of where our lives should be directed, and, above all, in understanding God. Language is what we use for thinking. Whoever is at the cutting edge in the development of new words and new symbols coerces society into thinking in certain directions. Given the wealth of scientific/technical/business/psychological jargon that permeates today's communications and the inability of our imitative Christian culture to generate contemporary, spiritually enriched symbols, we are left with the equivalent of a fifth-grade vocabulary to express immense theological realities. Anyone overhearing our fifth-grade talk surely must conclude that the spiritual realm is therefore made up of fifth-grade concepts—nice enough for vague assurances about some kind of continuity after death, if that is needed, but inadequate for serious consideration beyond religious sentiment. What kind of witness is that to a world of people whose eternal destinies are at stake? So the first reason I give for emphasizing language is a matter of effective evangelism and the salvation of souls thereby.

Fifth-grade vocabulary is sufficient for shopping and practical daily communications. It does, however, limit the landscape of knowledge and expression. Is there any reason we as individuals cannot go beyond it? If we cannot think that for which we have no words, let us coin new words. God is the God of abundance and complexity. If to enhance our knowledge of Him and to worship Him and to live a life that is in itself worship we need increasingly richer means of conveying our love, our delight, and our gratitude, let us find the means.

Our pinnacle experiences deserve full expression. Why should we not tap any appropriate language—verbal, visual, musical, poetic, and gestural—that God has made possible for us to use? We thereby can probe the wealth of experience beyond the mundane even while we are inevitably involved with the mundane. Thereby, the spiritual realm is brought close. It impinges upon common experience as the Holy Spirit connects the two.

WORKING THROUGH THE PHYSICAL ━━━━━━━━━━━━━━━━━━━━━█

Developing varied languages gives us the means to go beyond the physical without rejecting it. This is especially important to our considerations because, on the one hand, we know work involves the concrete existence and use of tools, objects, instruments, machines, material, and structures, while, on the other hand, we can conceive that something nonphysical is going on while we use the physical.

We do not want to be narrow-minded Christians, rejecting the physical as meaningless, especially since God created the physical realm. If we reject the physical as meaningful, we line ourselves up with the scientific materialist for whom a Rembrandt painting must be understood to be, at the most, so many grams of canvas and paint and of so many inches of graphic form but of no further value. Limiting acceptable data to the merely measurable does not explain the Rembrandt painting's significance. A pure materialist perspective is too narrow. It leaves out the highest achievements and experiences of mankind featured by every civilization since the dawn of human history.

Similarly, Christianity perceives everyday experiences to be abounding with higher levels of significance, sometimes of such consequence that they can include encounters with God. Christians are equipped to splice the experiences of the earth and its history with the eternal. As citizens of the kingdom of God, we can tap the rich resources of knowledge and experience from the realm beyond time while we are active in time.

OPAQUE AND TRANSPARENT ASPIRATIONS ━━━━━━━━━━━━━━━█

Unlike Hollywood movie portrayals of the spiritual realm, which invariably require multiple smoke machines, the actual dimensions of the spirit are more vivid than those of the physical. I have always liked C. S. Lewis's description of the increasing solidity of things the closer one gets to heaven as portrayed in the book *The Great Divorce*. In that work the representatives of heaven appear to possess intense clarity of form and color while visitors coming near to heaven from the outside look somewhat like phantoms—tenuous and somewhat smudgy, if not transparent.

How interesting that description is for the modern mind, aware as we are that there is far more space than mass even in the densest physical object we use. How interesting, too, is the possibility of the physical body being caught up into heaven without disturbing its equilibrium, as described by the apostle Paul.

> I shall go on to tell of visions and revelations granted by the Lord. I know a Christian man [the apostle Paul is referring to himself] who fourteen years ago (whether in the body or out of it, I do not know—God knows) was caught up as far as the third heaven. And I know this same man (whether in the body or out of it, I do not know—God knows) was caught up into paradise, and heard words so secret that human lips may not repeat them. (2 Corinthians 12:1–4 NEB)

These words of the apostle Paul are not presented as a biblical metaphor. They are given as history. I see no alternative but to reject them as delusions of grandeur or accept them as experiences of grandeur. Having read all of the apostle Paul's contributions to the New Testament, I am convinced that this tough-minded man is relating a fact. He did receive revelations from spiritual dimensions, either through leaving his body and coming back into it or by leaving the body altogether. There is no requirement that the body had to be left behind. The Bible does not permit us to deny the physical in favor of the spirit or the spirit in favor of the physical.

If we confine our thinking to merely the physical when thinking about our ambitions, we will be forced to consider it to be a matter of being rooted only in our chromosomes. This would require us to restrict ambition to the pursuit of wealth, fame, position, and power—the worldly perspective. This view is, for the most part, self-centered, and it is opaque. By that I mean that we cannot see through it. We cannot perceive any value or meaning beyond it itself. The products of such ambition must pass away. They have no capacity to last. When they go, nothing whatsoever remains.

In contrast, the biblical view of ambition is that it should be transparent. Happily, it is not an end in itself. Whatever is accomplished through our ambitions has direct translation into eternity. There we will perceive the products of our ambition lasting forever because they will be made of eternal stuff. This means many of the ordinary doings of our life are, in actuality, extraordinary. They take place in time and space and find their completion in heavenly dimensions.

This can happen because, in a very profound way, our work is part of who we are. In God's economy, as we accomplish our work, something good happens to us and something of value is brought into existence. A transference takes place between the physical world and the spiritual world whenever we take action. For example, Jesus stated that whoever received one of His disciples was doing that which was equal to receiving Jesus. He went further and said that receiving Jesus was equal to receiving the heavenly Father. This idea is amplified when Jesus went on to connect simple acts to heavenly rewards. Actions in time have their resonance in eternity.

> To receive you is to receive me, and to receive me is to receive the One who sent me. Whoever receives a prophet as a prophet will be given a prophet's reward, and whosoever receives a good man because he is a good man will be given a good man's reward. And if anyone gives so much as a cup of cold water to one of these little ones, because he is a disciple of mine, I tell you this: that man will assuredly not go unrewarded. (Matthew 10:40–42 NEB)

It is interesting to note that the act of receiving a person must be done in a way that is appropriate to who the person is. Our actions and our work must be fitting, not merely well-intentioned. The apostle Paul adds to the interconnectedness of the spiritual and physical with these remarkable words: "Whether you eat or drink, or whatever you do, do all to the glory of God" (1 Corinthians 10:31 RSV).

THE LORD'S SUPPER

The most vivid picture of this is seen in the Lord's Supper, when bread and wine become a pledge of our new relationship (covenant) with the Lord as well as an announcement of His presence. As I partake in Communion, I do not believe that anything magical happens. I eat bread and drink wine, but every time it is a fresh encounter with the presence of Jesus.

During Communion, there are two factual realities before me. The first is the food that is presented to me, bread, which I bite and chew and swallow, and wine, which I sip. The movements of my jaw and mouth and tongue plus sight, scent, and taste demonstrate to me that the wine and the bread are real.

The second factual reality is the presence of Jesus as I partake. What do I do in order to see that Jesus is there? What I do is to look at the bread and the wine, receive them, and eat them. They remain bread and wine, but when I eat I perceive Jesus because He Himself said, "This bread is my body." To see the bread is to see Jesus. He who said He is the truth and who pledged that He would be present is present, and we realize that presence by the action of participation. We perceive His presence in the breaking of the bread. The Holy Spirit in each of us, who Jesus sent to teach us and of whom Jesus said, "He will guide you to all truth," affirms us of the presence of our Savior.

Much of the world assumes that Christians receiving the bread and the wine during communion is of no more consequence than citizens saluting the flag on a patriotic holiday. In such instances, Americans remember past patriots, such as George Washington and Thomas Jefferson, with great fondness and appreciation. That is proper gratitude and important for the health of the nation. But as Christians, we are not merely reminding ourselves of our founder. Certainly we are remembering the past death of Jesus, but our founder is alive and dwelling within us, including the very moments we gather around the table. We encounter a resurrected Jesus, who is present in the church, so much so that He said, "Where two or three are gathered in my name, there I am in the midst of them" (Matthew 18:20 RSV). However, the Lord's Supper even goes beyond this "gathering in my name." It is so much more a serious gathering of Christians that the apostle Paul states there were those who were sick and also those who were dead because they treated this sacred meal unworthily (1 Corinthians 11:27–30). Actions in the physical realm affected the dimension of the spiritual, which in turn caused physical changes. At the table of the Lord, a circular embracement reaches into the dimensions of the spiritual and back into the physical.

When I leave the table of the Lord, with its remaining plate of bread and chalice of wine, I cannot encounter them elsewhere in their common use without seeing them differently. The loaf on the communion table changes how I see any loaf of bread. The wine changes how I see all wine. It becomes increasingly easy to see the extraordinary behind the display of the ordinary each day of our lives.

Rather than my everyday experiences becoming an obstacle to seeing God, the reverse happens. They become the stage for encountering God. Repentance in an ordinary day establishes my salvation in eternity. A glass of water given on a particular day receives rewards in heaven. Prayer in time harnesses spiritual power and changes events. Actions in time and space gain the response of heavenly beings. This liberates us to operate in the marketplace because we can make it mean more than it appears to be. We do not have to be intimidated. We can operate with confidence because God is present now. In fact, the marketplace could not exist without His being there. Regardless of how much corruption might be present, we can exploit it for God's purposes and our own growth.

JUDGMENT

The apostle Paul affirmed this elevation of the ordinary act and wrote that our works are of such value that they will be assessed by God Himself. He clarifies our understanding of all human effort with a graphic description of the specialized work of those involved with the church. Those who minister in the building up of the church are warned that such ambitions had better be established upon the sure foundation, Jesus Christ. He describes how those building efforts will be judged.

> The work that each man does will at last be brought to light; the day of judgment will expose it. For that day dawns in fire, and the fire will test the worth of each man's work. If a man's building stands, he will be rewarded; if it burns, he will have to bear the loss; and yet he will escape with his life, as one might from a fire. (1 Corinthians 3:12–15 NEB)

These words enlarge a great and consistent theme in the Bible, that our work will be judged and rewards will be gained. We are all called to use the gifts God has given to build something during the time we have been given, whether we are building churches or exercising hospitality. The person who has made no effort to concentrate on building arrives in eternity empty-handed.

The building we build in time will last for eternity or not at all. The rewards thereby lost or gained will indicate whether or not we have traded eternal treasure and genuine pleasure for shabby, temporary substitutes. Once again, our time impinges upon our eternity. The special feature of God's judgment is that it amplifies the importance of our work.

TRANSIENT ACHIEVEMENTS

The only work we possess is that which we are doing this moment. There is no way for us to make all our work present even if we have a collection of products we have produced. All we can do is recall past achievements. From our perspective, work is as transient as music, which has a fragile present reality in terms of whatever sound we hear in the current moment. To make sense of that sound, we are dependent upon the memory of what went on before. When the last chord has been struck, the music departs, leaving a pleasant memory but no music.

As the music has departed so have our achievements, as far as we are concerned. But they are not gone for God, who continuously sees every action in what to us is the past. We can take comfort that all our past accomplishments are preserved in the mind of God. This is a wonderful realization. We can be secure in knowing that the mind of God goes beyond memory, since remembrance is an activity of time. All our accomplishments are very much present in God. He preserves them all, but not as old artifacts. He preserves them for eternal consequence.

The Egyptians thought they could bring worldly treasures into eternity, but all their wealth ended up in the possession of thieves or museums. Egyptian civilization provided a large-scale demonstration that it is impossible to transfer the products of opaque ambition into spiritual territory. The only treasures we can bring into eternity are character, our relationship with God, and a lifetime of appropriate works.

These are the serious issues of life and of heaven. These are what genuine success is about. They are of such monumental consequence that we must be vigorous in our thinking about them and in translating our thinking into transparent achievements. If we are physically and emotionally healthy, our ambitions will drive us to achieve. That is a given. Whether we achieve genuine success is another matter, which is why we must make a sober estimate of what we are doing and why we are doing it. If we embrace a high view of humanity, we will perceive our ambitions to be among the highest gifts of all those God has folded into our beings.

THE PRACTICAL CONCLUSION

THE SECULAR CULTURAL VIEW

From the secular viewpoint, the world divides people into two categories, high achievers and low achievers. The high achievers are the usual inventory of the brilliant, the well-adjusted, the wealthy, the famous, the highly placed, and the important people. Conversely, the low achievers are those of average intelligence, the not-so-bright, those who never completed high school or college, those with low or average income, the unknown, those who are in ordinary jobs, and those who are not key players.

The reasons we are in one category or the other are legion. Fortune, birth, circumstances, opportunities, natural endowments, character, giftedness, emotional stability, economics, family values, and culture combine in complex ways to deliver an individual into one category or another. Where one draws the line between high and low achievers varies according to who is drawing the line. Ultimate meaning is achieving a place above the line in the hope that people will remember our efforts beyond our death.

THE DIVINE VIEW

Humans do not know who is or is not genuinely important. They are locked within a very narrow view of reality. They see only surfaces and are impressed with that which has transient value. They do not know that the presence or absence of wealth, education, fame, beauty, and power are all irrelevant to those who achieve the best in the end.

Humans do not have the slightest idea who is first and who is last in the kingdom of God. Most cannot see that a shriveled soul can reside behind a beautiful or handsome face. They do not see that the limitations of birth, education, money, neighborhood, and confinement in low-level jobs create no more or less distance between them and the highest attainments possible in the kingdom than do the reverse conditions. They do not know that the cashier at a diner who has embraced genuine humility can attain higher permanent status in eternity than the treasurer at a Fortune 500 company who knows the word *humility* but not its meaning. They do not realize that the prince has no greater capacity for joy than the peasant. They cannot perceive that even vast knowledge collapses in value before spiritual wisdom, that earthly fame is inconsequential, while God's "Well done thou good and faithful servant" is precious beyond telling.

Too many humans are ambitious to attain that which will eventually and surely bring them to the kingdom of darkness and reject the splendor that is available to those in the kingdom of light. Those who know the Light rejoice while they work, pray when they suffer, praise then they play, and wait patiently for the coming kingdom of which they are already citizens.

CHAPTER EIGHT

THE DESIGN LENS

The third lens through which we can look at ambition is through the design of persons and, in particular, our individual selves. In the world of design one often hears the principle: Form follows function. The design of an object, and indeed the beauty one can perceive in the design of an object, is dependent upon the purpose for which the object was made.

One does not craft a square spoon if it is to be used for eating purposes. We do not confuse the purpose of a jet airliner with that of an automobile. Only in a bizarre, imaginary world can one see a fleet of jumbo jets driving down Interstate 95. Survey the parts of an airplane and, even though one might not have ever seen one, it won't take long to surmise its use, if there is a basic familiarity with the technical world. Similarly, if we look at the design of a human being, we discover much that does not require anything but logic to reveal.

TWO FOUNDATIONAL VIEWS

When we look at the design of a person we encounter an array of interesting evidence about his or her nature. We begin with the realization that everyone who is human is derivative. No individual is self-created, and in fact each of our existences, yours and mine, was dependent upon the decisions of others (who were also not self-sufficient) in order to have come into existence.

Obviously, since the universe had a beginning and is also made up of stuff that is derivative, and we have never seen or experienced anything in the universe which is complete in itself, we must look elsewhere for our individual origin than the universe. Where do we look? We must look outside the universe to the One who created it. This can be an intellectual strain to those whose education has been wrapped up in scientific ideology. However, each of us must place our faith somewhere to make any sense out of our lives. There are two basic alternatives: either exclude God or include Him. For me, to exclude God is to choose that which is conceptually inferior. I take this position for three reasons.

1. *Intellectual history does not present a loftier or more inexhaustible concept than God.* The idea of God is the most sophisticated, brilliant concept that has ever crossed the mind of man. Though science is fascinating, no concept encountered so far in any of the sciences equals the breadth and the depth of the Judeo-Christian understanding of God.

Since science relegates itself to the phenomena of the universe, it must necessarily be contained by it. This is a narrower view than those who hold that there is more than that which is created, which, in turn, suggests that there is more to human life than existence.

2. *Theology perceives that a personal God is not only an appropriate source for human personality, but presents an extraordinarily high view of it.* Any other conclusion is inadequate, especially when it reduces love, imagination, self-identity, art, and intelligence to biochemical activities of the brain.

3. *Since the dawn of time, high views of God have engendered great painting, architecture, literature, and music.* Atheism and agnosticism are not very festive and do not inspire creativity. Civilizations where low views of God prevail tend to be low in artistic achievement. The more technical the society the more boring the aesthetic. The church produces feasts. Science produces vitamin tablets. This suggests greater richness in human potential than mere socioeconomic considerations can justify.

Given the above, I can understand the apostle Paul's attributing the rejection of the idea of God (to say nothing of rejecting God Himself) as a symptom of wickedness. The apostle Paul would accuse many in our scientific communities of being idolaters, attributing the wonders of the universe to sources so inferior to God that the distance between God and their theories is like the distance between Jehovah and primitive idols of wood and stone.

> For we see divine retribution revealed from heaven and falling upon all godless wickedness of men. In their wickedness they are stifling the truth. For all that may be known of God by men lies plain before their eyes; indeed God himself has disclosed it to them. His invisible attributes, that is to say his everlasting power and deity, have been visible, ever since the world began, to the eye of reason, in the things he has made. There is therefore no possible defence for their conduct; knowing God, they have refused to honour him as God, or to render him thanks. Hence all their thinking has ended in futility, and their misguided minds are plunged in darkness. (Romans 1:18–21 NEB)

Man perceived physically is fascinating. Man perceived physically and spiritually is astounding. It is foundational to the understanding of one's own personhood to realize that as soon as we connect our existence to that of God, everything shifts into a higher gear, especially when we attempt to gain an understanding of our ambitions. It becomes simultaneously an individual and divine matter and charges the issue with great significance.

CHAPTER NINE

SEEING HUMAN DESIGN

T he opening chapters of this book displayed the varieties of intentions people display in accomplishing something more than survival. If the human race were designed only to maintain existence, our civilization could be described totally in economic terms. What actually happens is that once survival is achieved creative efforts appear and expand. Those efforts involve both the physical and the spiritual capabilities of personality.

We are equipped with physical bodies designed to perform a prodigious variety of tasks. As individuals, we not only are physically shaped with amazing precision, but in organizations and communities we are capable of orchestrating great diversities of gifts. We thereby bring together the vast variety of physical and conceptual capabilities necessary for building and sustaining civilizations.

Given the panorama of those civilizations over thousands of years, it is astonishing to realize that there are those who believe it all adds up to nothing. When we look at the design of our humanity through the humanity of Jesus Christ we get an entirely different picture.

HUMAN DESIGN

The company I lead has been involved in equipping organizations to make good decisions about the effective leadership and management of their people, plus assisting many individuals in their career development. Our files are filled with thousands of reports providing detailed analysis of the gifted abilities individuals bring to their work and careers. Our conclusion is not only that God has designed each person in detail with very particular strengths to achieve very specific results, but that every person is uniquely gifted. Any attempt to affix simplistic labels on people is a serious error.

A person cannot be rammed into a box, grid, or graph without distorting our understanding of that individual. This conclusion flies in the face of much of what the world has assumed for all the years of my education. However, it is in harmony with some of the conclusions now emerging from new research that concludes that people are indeed unique.

Christians give the idea of uniqueness much allegiance in terms of official biblical belief, but in practice they have assumed what the world has assumed. Current management, leadership, and human resource policies and practices in most Christian organizations support this conclusion, bringing confusion to employees attempting to understand what they are to do in life.

If people do not know that they are designed in great detail in terms of what they are motivated and gifted to accomplish, they are going to assume they can do anything. However, a high percentage of those who have tried "anything" have ended up accomplishing little that was satisfying to them, whether or not they were competent. This just perpetuates the confusion, which is how we end up with preachers who cannot preach, managers who do not manage, leaders who cannot come up with a vision, and organizers who cannot organize.

Given this chaotic state, the best approach to negotiate our way through the confusion would be to look at an ideal example. We use Jesus Christ for this purpose. In doing so, we are not presenting Him as a model of what particular gifts we should have. That is a decision God has already made in creating each of us. We use Jesus as the best example of ultimate success according to the principles He established in His ministry on earth. He is a model of how a human being can express life in a fallen world. This, then, is for those who "have put on the new nature, which is constantly renewed in the image of its Creator and brought to know God" (Colossians 3:10 NEB).

JESUS CHRIST

HIS WORK

Is not this the carpenter? (Mark 6:3 NEB)

Like the apostle Paul, learned man that he was, yet who was able to earn his own way through the tent-making trade, Jesus was also associated with a trade, in this case being a carpenter. Jesus took a role in life that most of us must take on, and that is the role of a worker. God has equipped us to do work that is of service to others. Tent-making and working with wood were not spiritual activities, but both the apostle Paul and Jesus make clear that ordinary work is of value.

HIS GIFTS

A sentimental view of Jesus' natural gifts was that He had all the gifts. That does not fit the idea of Jesus being a man of like passions as we, facing human limitation like any other man. Neither does it fit the biblical evidence. His teaching gifts, His mentoring abilities, His attractive way of enticing individuals to the truth, His creative metaphors and parables, and His influencing and ministry abilities are all vivid displays of particular strengths with which He was gifted in His humanity.

We too have been given natural gifts with which to bless others through their exercise. Jesus displayed these gifts early as a child in the temple, and, like Him, we will find that our gifts began to emerge in childhood. We will discover that we do with greater sophistication now that which we were gifted to do as children.

We need to follow our bent, to be what God has equipped us to be. He has not done this in some vague way, but has designed into us richly detailed capabilities. We need to express those capabilities through the skills that fit them. This is where training and education come in. They provide the opportunity to develop those skills that permit the most effective expression of our gifts. That opens the way to serve others through competence.

HIS MISSION

> I have glorified thee on earth by completing the work which thou gavest me to do; and now, Father, glorify me in thy own presence with the glory which I had with thee before the world began. (John 17:4–5 NEB)

This prayer is a culminating moment in the life of Jesus as He surveys all He has done and is about to do on the Cross. He concludes that it all has glorified His Father. The work of Jesus demonstrated God's glory.

One feature of God's glory on earth is that it is a means for others to apprehend the presence of God. Glory is a visible demonstration of the reality of God, who is otherwise hidden in ultimate mystery. The work that God gave His Son to do was a means for the world to connect with the reality of God. Similarly, the work, the attitude, and the relationship of Jesus' coworkers—His disciples— glorified Jesus and thereby made the presence of the Son of God real to people.

> And glory has come to me through them. (John 17:10 NIV)

This glory went far beyond a display of Jesus' reputation in comparison to other prophets. The effect of this glory was to stimulate sinners to look to Jesus for truth and healing of the body, mind, and spirit. It focused empty hearts upon the power and truth of Jesus as the Redeemer. We who are also Christ's disciples can bring glory to Jesus through our jobs, our ministry, and our service. We thereby make Him real to others who observe what we do.

Jesus' work of ministry was a short term mission. It was sacrificial because it required the denial of natural human hopes and ambitions for the sake of sinners. So we too need to take on mission tasks for the sake of others. They will all be temporary tasks because once we are beyond time there will be no further need for mission activities. Then tasks which fit our gifts will be the norm and our pleasure. Meanwhile, we have the responsibility to make sure others will come to enjoy the same pleasure.

For some, the congruence of their gifts, ambitions, and mission will place them in a position where most of their earthly time will be given to ministry. All of us, however, ought to be available for ministry or service as soon as we see a need that fits our capabilities or even one that merely requires labor.

HIS GOAL

From time to time each of us is likely to survey the work we have accomplished so far in life. How shall we measure its quality? It would seem from Jesus' survey of His life's work that success was attained when the Father's will was satisfied and glory had been achieved.

What is of special interest was that glory was manifested in both natural and unnatural work. The natural work was that for which Jesus was gifted. His effectiveness in developing leaders and equipping them to minister and establish the church is confirmed. The church still continues centuries after she was first founded. All of this fits Jesus' natural gifts.

The unnatural work was to take on the roles of the Suffering Servant, the sacrificial lamb. He who knew divine freedom was nailed to a cross. He who was the source of life was tortured and killed. The inconceivable took place, all of it abysmally unnatural but necessary.

It was necessary if we were to be rescued from death and meaninglessness. Jesus took on His dual role by performing both His natural and unnatural tasks so that they brought glory to the Father. We who are called to follow in the footsteps of Jesus are called to apply our natural gifts to natural jobs. But while we do that, we can expect from time to time to be given sacrificial tasks, ones that do not fit us. We are to fulfill such tasks with the same joy as those that do fit us and also bring glory to God.

PART THREE

GAINING A SHARPER FOCUS

I have chosen Bezalel, son of Uri, the son of Hur, . . . and I have filled him with the Spirit of God, with skill, ability and knowledge in all kinds of crafts—to make artistic designs for work in gold, silver and bronze, to cut and set stones, to work in wood, and to engage all kinds of craftsmanship.

Exodus 31:1–5 NASB

Nothing is really work unless you would rather be doing something else.

J. M. Barrie

Blessed is he who has found his work, let him ask no other blessedness.

Thomas Carlyle

CHAPTER TEN

AMBITION

ince ambition is a characteristic of personality, every person is ambitious in some way. But since each person has a unique personality, every person has different ambitions. Aside from those whose motivations have been crippled through pathology, it is a mistake to believe that some people are ambitious while others are not. Such ideas have developed as a reaction to the contrast between those whose ambitions urge high visibility and line up with cultural standards of success and those whose ambitions keep them in a supportive role. Some people in the latter category are not only disinterested in what success is popularly perceived to be, but reject it altogether as a meaningless value.

ANALYZING THE STEWARDSHIP OF AMBITION

Whereas ambition operates in a unique manner in each person, there are four components I use in assisting people to analyze the quality of their stewardship as it relates to their ambitions. They are presented here somewhat in priority order:

VALUES

By this I mean the assumptions that are foundational in a person's life, enabling him to make some kind of sense out of his existence or to realize a meaningful purpose for living. These may be informal and have emerged out of the subculture in which the individual was reared. Or they may be derived from philosophy or out of religious training or an experience with God. Sometimes values are a simple justification for a preferred lifestyle, bad or good.

What needs to be emphasized here is that *the source of a person's values will determine the kind of power that will ignite his ambition.* The degree of power equals the determination with which an individual will pursue objectives that express his or her values.

> Example: Jim grew up in Dallas, where his father has had outstanding success in business. Jim has made it his aim in life to duplicate his father's goals of establishing a family in town and owning a ranch in the country for leisure. All Jim's education and career plans were driven by these simple goals, which expressed the values of his family.
>
> Then Jim had a serious encounter with values that are rooted in the Bible. He began to ask himself questions he had never before considered. "What does a family mean?" "What about a ranch is worth achieving?" "Do my gifts fit business?" "Does God have a claim on what I do with my life?" "What would please God?" "Why would that please Him?" Now that he is attempting to answer these questions, he is dumbfounded that such queries had never before occurred to him. He had never critiqued his own cultural assumptions but merely assumed them as a foundation for existence. He never thought outside the context of his own family environment.

There is nothing inherently wrong with the values with which Jim was brought up, but the question is whether they were the best for him. The biblical perspective condemns any value system that compromises the best. We are directed to seek those values that are of ultimate worth. They are portrayed in the Bible but need to be developed in a personal relationship with the God who knows what will ultimately and always satisfy.

OBJECTIVES

Our foundational values will be translated into achievable objectives. For some this will happen organically, with each decision opening up the potential for future opportunities. For others it needs to be planful, with clearly stated specific objectives. Either approach needs to be accompanied by prayer.

For those who prefer to operate with anticipated goals, it might be useful to recognize several levels of objectives. The first is *vision,* which involves the imagination open to the Holy Spirit so we might gain a picture of who and what we hope to become.

The second level of objectives is seen in terms of the *mission.* The mission is comprised of specific results to be brought about that conform to the vision. It may be a goal to be achieved at the end of a particular phase of living (Earn a college degree. Attain a real estate license) or it might be a career goal (Become a medical missionary. Become a teacher. Become a farmer).

The third level involves the kind of *consistent results* the individual is motivated to bring about. These results are particular goals which need to be attained in a project or activity that is motivationally meaningful for the individual. They determine how a person will go about achieving his work and service.

> Examples: Some people want to attain higher degrees of expertise, whereas others are driven to build or develop something. Some people want to lead, whereas others are motivated to create new concepts. One individual wants to overcome obstacles; another wants to make an impact on others.

Ordinarily, for anyone's life to be fulfilled, these three levels of results must be achieved *harmoniously.* Suppose a person can satisfy his or her values in a farming career. Assuming such an individual is also motivated to build and develop, it would be a mistake to take a permanent position on a large corporate farming operation that has already been built. It would be better to own or lease land and develop one's own operation. Because it would necessarily be smaller, that would dictate what production could be, given market considerations.

The reverse would be true of someone interested in farming but who is motivated to attain higher degrees of expertise. That individual could work on a large operation, but only one in which farming technology had not only been honed, but in which new developments were always in the works to maximize productivity or to expand diversity. That would assure a built-in continuum of learning and training.

MOTIVATED GIFTS

These are the specific sets of skills and capabilities that an individual consistently brings to his work. They enable an individual to achieve his objectives.

Examples: Organizing information, analyzing data, negotiating political issues, persuading audiences, innovating programs, probing problems, developing systems, designing programs.

CONTEXT

These are the conditions that support consistent performance or gaining particular results. Conditions that fit one person annoy another. The context can be physical, managerial, or environmental. These elements and some examples for each are listed below.

- Physical: Outdoors, international, urban
- Managerial: Independence, measures of success, specifications, challenges, close management
- Environmental: Pressure, creative, structured, competitive

The *context* plus *gifts* plus *consistent results* are all factors of individual giftedness. Long-term study indicates that they are permanent in nature, so they do not change in kind though they are used in more skillful ways as people mature.

In practice, these four categories work, for the most part, as a unity. The artifice of labeling them here is to provide a way to analyze and evaluate what otherwise might seem too complex to understand or to manage. That analysis will display the wonderful peculiarity of an individual's aspirations.[1]

AMBITION REQUIRES FREEDOM ———————————————■

The Gospel of Jesus Christ is radical. God does not change us by mere indoctrination. The Gospel is driven home by the Holy Spirit, who not only convinces us of truth, but goes on to make us capable of receiving it into our lives and have our motivations revolutionized. Only the Holy Spirit is able to free us from the imprisonment of massaging our egos long enough to look to Jesus Christ, who loved us first and who proved it in the most convincing manner one can conceive.

Once we are willing to come into a relationship with Christ, we can become "new creatures in Christ," to use a phrase from the apostle Paul. Our history remains intact, but we are free to be the unique persons God intended us to be rather than blindly conforming to what our subculture, education, or friends need and expect us to be.

We must be careful to protect this freedom, for as soon as the signals of this liberty are seen, certain legalistic religious people, who are not necessarily spiritual, make their appearance. They are not well-informed by a holistic view of the Bible, though they present themselves as knowledgeable in the Scriptures. They exploit isolated verses taken out of context to coerce us into a new prison house of rules and religious effort, especially when it comes to the subject of what you should be doing with your life.

Freedom, especially somebody else's, makes them nervous. Instead of encouraging us to establish beachheads in the marketplace, they hide behind their chapel barriers repeating the gospel over and over to those who have already heard. They are intimidated by the world and cannot speak in terms a potential convert can understand.

Above all, they insist on conformity to their rules, which provides them the illusion of unity—but not the unity brought about by the Holy Spirit. Theirs is actually political unity in a religious setting. It isn't the unity of God's people, whom the Scriptures describe in Acts 2 as being with one accord in one place when the Holy Spirit fell on them and inspired them to speak in a *variety* of languages. Clearly the unity brought about by the Holy Spirit in the birth of the church was not fragile. It flourished even when everyone was speaking differently; it was a unity with many different expressions, a unity that delighted in diversity.

God's unity is multicolored, with and inclusive of a great variety of forms. Look at the unity of the earth with its myriad varieties of life-forms, from the single-cell paramecium all the way up to the unfathomable complexities of the human brain. All of it is unified by God through precise, many-layered symbiotic systems. He holds it all securely together.

If we listen to the Holy Spirit, He informs us that we are the children of God, who are unified with Him. Jesus did everything necessary to place us in that position, and we cannot improve it. That is why the church can unleash all her people on the world, with all their different gifts, working in high jobs and low jobs, in all kinds of professions and organizations, serving mankind and telling everywhere by word and deed who Jesus is without worrying about how it is all going to hold together—especially when it happens in the marketplace, where the church doesn't have control. The church's responsibility is to equip her people and set their ambitions free to accomplish service and the work of the ministry outside the church and in the world.

AMBITION REQUIRES SANCTIFICATION

Unless there is an intersection in our lives with the life of Jesus Christ, our ambitions remain compulsively self-centered and preoccupied with dramatizing our own importance and uniqueness. Jesus, who is the quintessential individualist, free to be Himself as no other human being before or after, takes on the goal of freeing us from this self-centered preoccupation because it will kill the very thing we intend to preserve.

Jesus gives away His own life with its ambitions to save us from ourselves. That is the meaning of the Cross. He gives us the power to give ourselves away to serve others as He served us. He enables us to choose freedom, to become the unique persons He designed us to be, not the persons the world would have us imitate.

> No man is worthy of me who does not take up his cross and walk in my footsteps. By gaining his life a man will lose it; by losing his life for my sake, he will gain it. (Matthew 10:38–39 NEB)

SANCTIFICATION REJECTS THE MATERIAL AS THE ULTIMATE GOAL

Ambition spontaneously triggers us into action by focusing upon a result or a goal. A person who is locked within the limitations of the physical world can look no further than things, money, power, and fame as worthy goals. That is all the world talks about. That is what countless books, magazines, television programs, songs, and movies of all kinds are preoccupied with, though nothing on that list has any intrinsic or permanent value. None of them is valuable in itself. They are neither bad nor good; they are only mediums through which we can get things done.

They can be bad or good for us, but that depends upon our individual character, not our inherent qualities. Those who have chosen to believe that the physical is everything and that there is nothing beyond appearances are in trouble. They have placed their faith in the ultimate value of that which has never proven to be of anything but temporary use to anyone. They have also chosen the least interesting option, which should in itself be a clue to how wrong the path is they have taken.

SANCTIFICATION REJECTS THE SPIRITUAL AS AN APPROPRIATE GOAL

Self-centered ambitions are voracious in their appetites. It makes no difference to people with ambitions of this type whether they do or do not attain materialistic or spiritual objectives as long as they get their own way. They surmise the spiritual arena is just as good as the material, as long as their egos are in the driver's seat. Here are several types of these spiritually ambitious people.

1. *People who, without necessarily using the word* spiritual, *have a desire for other "forces" to be operative in their lives and bring about changes in some way.* People who involve themselves with horoscopes are a prime example of this. They do not usually have any philosophical thoughts about life strategy, just a hope that other forces, even stars, might cooperate with their ambitions to bring about that for which their hearts long.

Rationality is the best protection against this inclination, but given its characteristic absence in these people, they display less and less ability to engage the astringent, intense clarity they need and which is found in common sense and truth.

2. *People who are intrigued by the occult, often in terms of its magical power, but do not understand the forces behind that magic.* These people may dabble in the occult from time to time with seances, cards, or other paraphernalia, so that they can achieve their ambitions without work or effort. They are either fascinated with the future and what it will bring or are eager to see a demonstration of some kind of spiritual reality or magical knowledge.

This is inevitable in a time such as ours. Since we are in an age devoted to technology, there is a consequent absence of spiritual nurture. Because people are not only physical but spiritual in nature, they don't do well when only one part of them is being fed, so they range about for some kind of spiritual food. Uninstructed by truth, or in outright willfulness, such people encounter and embrace evil spirits masquerading as good entities, who, if the truth be known, are looking at them as food. Some spiritually hungry people see behind the masks but nevertheless commit themselves completely to satanic cults. They end up believing in the spiritual realm but serve a different father than the one the Christian serves. They become declared enemies of truth, especially as it appears in the Gospel of Jesus Christ, and they are committed to its demise.

3. *People who are spiritually ambitious and interested in biblical truth, and who are often knowledgeable about spiritual things and are possibly genuine Christians (or began as Christians), but whose true emphasis is worldly ambition.* These people certainly can talk the language. They enjoy being looked upon as knowledgeable and they love exercising spiritual authority over others, but they love it for its own sake. In other words, what we have are classic worldly ambitions in the guise of spiritual authority and often in the office of spiritual authority.

The best example of inordinate spiritual ambition is the story of Simon in the book of Acts. Simon had a career in the magical arts and had "swept the Samaritans off their feet" (Acts 8:9 NEB) with his powerful displays. Philip came along and preached the Gospel, with highly successful results. Many miracles took place. As a result of Philip's ministry, a great number of Samaritans were baptized in water, including Simon. In fact, the Scriptures indicate that Simon spent all his time close to Philip and his company.

When the apostles in Jerusalem heard what was happening in Samaria they sent Peter and John to follow up Philip's ministry. Peter and John arrived and laid hands on those who had been converted and baptized so that they could receive the Holy Spirit. When Simon saw this, he was amazed and attempted to buy this spectacular gift from the apostles, so that "when I lay my hands on anyone, he will receive the Holy Spirit." Peter's response was not gentle.

> Your money go with you to damnation, because you thought God's gift was for sale! You have no part nor lot in this, for you are dishonest with God. Repent of this wickedness and pray the Lord to forgive you for imagining such a thing. I can see that you are doomed to taste the bitter fruit and wear the fetters of sin. (Acts 8:20–24 NEB)

Simon was an expert in magic, and he knew an authentic performance when he saw it. It was clear that his offer to Peter and

John was driven by the ambition to be in a position of power. He wanted spiritual reality to serve his ambitions. The fierceness of Peter's response probably surprised Simon, who now was encountering what was to him a new thing, the ambitions of men at the service of spiritual reality.

Jesus gave more than one warning about inappropriate spiritual ambition. Here is one of His more unsettling statements:

> Not everyone who calls me 'Lord, Lord' will enter the kingdom of Heaven, but only those who do the will of my heavenly Father. When that day comes, many will say to me, 'Lord, Lord, did we not prophesy in your name, cast out devils in your name, and in your name perform many miracles?' Then I will tell them to their face, 'I never knew you; out of my sight, you and your wicked ways!' (Matthew 7:21–23 NEB)

What is interesting here is that there is no indication that the many miracles were fake. They probably were real. God may exploit someone's ministry for the sake of those who are being ministered to, but that does not necessarily authenticate the one doing the ministering. The ambition to be a famous preacher or prophet or miracle worker can be as empty as the worldly brand of fame. But to exercise those gifts in humility, aware of who gave the gifts and who energizes them and for what purpose, is an ambition that gladdens the heart of God.

SANCTIFICATION FOCUSES UPON GOD AS THE APPROPRIATE GOAL

God is not closest to the one who has the highest view of Scripture or the most effective ministry, or the one who is wisest about the things of God. God is closest to those who are obedient, not because they earn the right through their works, but because they not only love God, but embody that love in action. Their love is passionate. It is love that is articulated in praise and ends in definitive acts.

What begins as a response to the voice of God grows in faith and knowledge and bursts into the exuberance of good works. God, who lives in the passionate love of the Trinity, is pleased by the passionate love of an individual's love toward Him. This is not because God requires it. That would be absurd. God gives us His love.

We need it. God loved us first and thereby imputed value to us, establishing the possibility of created individuals relating to the uncreated. It is a relationship that is not legal or theological, but personal. That is why this new relationship is such good news. It is open to anyone, not restricted to those who are credentialed by spiritual sensitivity or theological knowledge.

What is the end of this relationship with God? What do we find in it? An invitation to a meal.

> O taste and see that the Lord is good: blessed is the man that trusteth in him. (Psalm 34:8 KJV)

> My Father gives you the real bread from heaven. The bread that God gives comes down from heaven and brings life to the world. . . . I am the bread of life. Whoever comes to me shall never be hungry, and whoever believes in me shall never be thirsty. (John 6:32–35 NEB)

There is no desire and no ambition that does not have roots in the good things God has enabled us to enjoy. When we are hungry for anything—whether it be physical, intellectual, aesthetic, emotional, or spiritual—we have encountered an appetite that has at its base a God-invented desire. Every God-invented desire has a corresponding God-invented satisfaction. What Jesus is saying is that in His humanity He knows the desires of our bodies and hearts. He looks at us and surveys our hungers. He reviews the eternal wonders from which He was eternally begotten and out of that wealth offers the highest, the most sublime, the most ecstatic satisfaction there can be.

He turns to us and says, "Come to me. I know all your longings. I know all your hungers. You will never be hungry or thirsty again. I am the one for whom you are longing, I am the goal of all your ambitions. I am your ultimate satisfaction."

NOTE

1. A more detailed description of motivated gifts and context is available in the book *Visions of Grandeur,* by Ralph Mattson, a Praxis book, published by Moody Press; or write: The DOMA Group, Box 91, Canton Center, CT 06020, and request a more detailed description of human giftedness.

CHAPTER ELEVEN

mbition expresses itself in action, and this action we call
work. An example of this was the morning I rearranged a
section of the garden. I dug, moved large stones, and
transferred piles of dirt, sand, and peat. I strained and labored hour
after hour in the sun on a project I was not required to do, for a
reward that was solely in my head. There was no one to remunerate
me, no one to applaud my efforts, yet I plodded on, quite pleased
with the whole effort.

My objective was quite clear. In my mind's eye I saw the picture of what I intended to bring about. I knew I would increase the
beauty of my surroundings and provide increasing satisfaction for
many summers to come as the plantings matured and become a
visually unified whole. All of this, though beneficial, was unnecessary. There was no gaping hole in the landscape that needed to be
covered, since I was rearranging a portion of the garden that was
already planted. There was no one who had criticized what was
formerly there, suggesting that I ought to do something about
changing it. There was only an idea that grew in my head as I
scanned the garden and made a decision to execute my improve-
ment project. Once the decision was made, I planned, assembled

the necessary tools, made some improvements of the original plan as I worked, and finally brought it all to completion.

What is most useful to understand about this project is that it featured hard work that was not required. Because there was no compelling external imperative, one might assume the project was unimportant. However, I knew that I was not going to let much get in the way of completing it. This had my initials all over it. It was a personal matter that not only had me intensely focused upon the goal but also optimistic in the expectation that the goal would surely be achieved.

This behavior is not some peculiarity restricted to me. It is characteristic of the human race. Consider all the time and energy poured into amateur athletic activities of all kinds on any given day. It involves millions of people of all ages, but very little of it is a genuine necessity. Only a small number of participants are driven primarily by the need for exercise. There are those who will leave a physically demanding job at the end of the day only to use their remaining daylight hours participating in a physically demanding softball game.

In some foundational way, my exertions as a landscaper and those of the softball player running the bases are similar. Our efforts are wonderfully uncessary.

Somewhere, someone is right now assembling a wonderful culinary masterpiece that is destined to do more than take care of someone's need for vitamins. Somewhere else children are gathering materials to build a tree house, a project that has yet to attract the enthusiasm of their parents but which will be completed no matter how many negotiations need to take place.

A friend of mine has been running many miles each day to prepare for a future race that, it is very clear to me, he does not have to run. He has a different opinion. When I ask him about it, I realize that from his perspective he must run it. His wife makes beautiful quilts that will not be used by them. They have all the blankets and quilts they need.

The cook, the children, the runner, and the quilter are all doing what is not required by anyone else but themselves. Every one of them has a picture in his or her mind of what he or she wants to achieve, and each of them will press forward until it is attained. It all represents work, but not in terms of how we usually view work.

The reason I picked these particular examples is because they all involve work without external coercion. Salaries, survival, and career development are not involved here. None of these projects adds to the economy. They are done for their own sake, for reasons that are uniquely personal and not necessarily related to practicality.

Why I take this approach is to demonstrate that work, which is usually conceived of as an economic necessity, makes its appearance even when there is no economic demand. This is to correct the idea that work is a result of the Fall from paradise or the idea that when we get to heaven we will no longer work, but spend all our time singing long choral compositions.

Perhaps I would tell a questioning child that work in heaven is a pleasure to do, like play or like hobbies. Hobbies are an interesting phenomenon because they are what we do when our careers do not sufficiently satisfy our motivational interests. If we cannot satisfy in our jobs what we are ambitious to do, we attain satisfaction outside our employment. When one is motivated to spend more time on outside activities than on the job, it sends a clear message that there is something wrong, not necessarily with the quality or the benefits of the job, but likely with the job-fit or its potential for contributing to the goals of one's ambition.

We must separate the action of work from the reason for work. One is work, the other ambition. If we look at work as the means to satisfy ambition, it can help us be sensible in the stewardship of our lives and talents.

INCARNATING OUR AMBITION INTO WORK

In chapter 5 we saw that the presence of our ambitions, regardless of how humble or grand they may appear to be, is a reflection of God's "ambition" (remembering that that is not an entirely satisfying word to describe what moves God into action). We are motivated to accomplish because He has made us that way. Because ambition makes no sense until it translates into achievements, each of us expresses his ambitions through some form of work. We need to see certain results if we are to feel content about our efforts.

We are like lovers, who are not satisfied merely to experience the emotional sensation of love but who are compelled to express and act out their love. The particular expression we choose should fit the nature of that love. What is appropriate in one loving relationship is not fitting for another. Similarly, the work we do should fit the ambitions we have.

Translating our ambitions into work can be confusing. One obstacle may be pathology. We have all encountered people who talk about their ambitions but who seem unable to take the first steps toward actualizing that vision. Sometimes this is due to some kind of damage within their personalities which blocks the development of confidence. Or perhaps there is a crippling condition within an individual's spirit that absorbs all the energy that would otherwise be devoted to achieving a healthy form of success. Or their hesitation may simply be due to a flaw in their character.

If ever we find ourselves with any of these symptoms, we should waste no time in seeking out the assistance of those who are gifted to help us. This is too serious a matter to let such conditions continue and allow our lives to drift aimlessly. No one was ever created by God for a meaningless and aimless existence.

A second obstacle to translating our ambitions into appropriate work is errant thinking. There are two mistakes that affect how we go about achieving long-term success, given the healthiest meaning of that word. The first is to buy into the secular view of a person as a kind of commodity. In spite of the description of gifts given in previous chapters, we may yet see ourselves as a kind of raw material, like clay, to be shaped into whatever society or our family needs us to be or what we want ourselves to be. The correction to the inclination to be a "commodity" is found in chapters 8 and 9.

Another error is to assume that institutions can make us into what we want to be. We tend to place great confidence in law schools to produce lawyers and seminaries to produce pastors and business schools to produce entrepreneurs. I certainly do not share that confidence, having been involved with hundreds upon hundreds of misplaced professionals who, unfortunately, made that assumption. Professional institutions will credential anyone who has fulfilled their requirements, but lawyers, pastors, and entrepreneurs who are successful in their careers have more than institutional certification. Unlike their less fulfilled peers who also have institutional certification, they had the appropriate gifts to bring to the professional training. As a result, the gifts and the training combined to enable them to enjoy the achievements of their careers.

A CHALLENGE

Some Christians challenge this view. They believe God could call us into any kind of work according to His will, even in spite of our preferences, and then provide us satisfaction by converting our former disinterest into a passion. With God, they say, anything can happen, anything is possible. That, of course, is not quite true. Although we certainly cannot put God into a box, neither ought we to assume a simplistic view of how He operates. God is limited by His own nature. By that I mean He cannot do what God by nature doesn't do. God is also sovereign, but that doesn't mean anything can happen. It means God has absolute authority, and He exercises that authority in a manner consistent with who He is. When He encounters an individual, He addresses someone whom He—and nobody else—designed and made in highly complex detail. He does not violate that design in how He relates to a person, nor does He change His mind about His creation. God must work in harmony with that which He authors.

Unlike humans, God does not have a future where He learns something that would cause Him to change what He did in His past. As already stated, God does not dwell in time. Time exists in God; He is not subject to time. Occasionally, the Old Testament describes God as changing His mind because of bad behavior by individuals or nations (see, for example, Jeremiah 18:10). People (who do have a future) are vulnerable to changes on God's part when they make decisions requiring it. But none of these changes remotely fits the idea of God making changes in how He designed each individual. People who have been gifted by God with a rich array of technical gifts, but no speaking or communicating gifts, will not be called to lay down their technical tools to conduct evangelistic crusades. They will not awaken some morning fluent as a Billy Graham.

GOD'S ACTION IS COMPLETE ACTION

God's process in making us did not cease the moment we were conceived. We originated in the mind of God. He saw us before we were conceived. He brought us into existence and gave us being. He continues to do so today and will always do so. All of His actions toward us are informed by His complete knowledge of how He designed us. When God addresses me, He addresses me as man because that is what He made me, and I do not expect any changes in that status. When He ordained my birth, He thereby assured that I live now. I am not going to be removed into a past period of time even if I preferred it. God deals with me in terms of my current state of intellectual and emotional development, according to the facts of my history and according to the spiritual maturity I have attained. He is able to do so because He was involved with every one of those aspects of who I am. His Holy Spirit is present in all my times, and within me since conversion. He is not going to install changes that are not in harmony with how He made me, as if I were a robot that could be upgraded. It would be one thing if we made ourselves, in which case we could remake ourselves to fit what is currently convenient for us, but the Scripture says otherwise.

It is he that hath made us, and not we ourselves. (Psalm 100:3 KJV)

As a teenager hearing that Scripture, I was surprised that such an obvious fact needed to be stated. Given current culture, I can see why it was. The full implications of this verse desperately need to be understood by the world and the church.

God always addresses us as the unique creations He made us to be. That is the first call in our lives—to be what He ordained us to be for all time. God is not a God of confusion, making us one thing and calling us to another. God will not call someone to a permanent position of misfit work that has nothing to do with who He made that person to be, even if that work is a ministry. Circumstances may, at times, require it, but not because God desired it, no more than He desires that fatal accidents take place or that tragedies befall us.

Misfit work affects one's physical and emotional health. That has become increasingly clear, given the research now being done evaluating how job misfit, health, and productivity affect each other. The data is appalling in its conclusions. Apparently God does not give us bodies and minds that can take activities that do not fit them for any lengthy period of time without damaging them.

APPROPRIATE WORK

Ambition and work become congruent in the discovery of our purpose and in good career and job-fit. It is easy in our fragmented society to focus on one separately from the other. This is why most people do not know what they are doing in these matters. It is why many Christians abdicate their responsibilities by "turning it all over to God," by which they mean, "I don't know how to deal with this."

It is one thing to exercise faith regarding our future; it is another to practice escapism or to plod along, doing whatever turns up. We are not called to a haphazard life, but an obedient life. We are to accept who God created us to be, responsible in the use of our gifts both spiritual and natural and willing to take an appropriate place in our community. Here are the basics in thinking biblically about these matters.

THE GOD WHO WORKS: THE INVENTOR OF WORK

The most foundational fact to have in our heads is that the God of the Bible works. As previously stated, God is not static, but dynamic, and has produced at least one product we know about, the universe with us in it.

This is a universe that gives all the measurable signals of that which is not self-generating, but has instead emerged by the action of God, who is not Himself a part of the universe. The opening words of the Bible portray the God who works: "In the beginning God created heaven and earth." It then goes on to present the fascinating story of how He did that, ending with God resting when He came to the end of His work.

> On the seventh day God ended his work which he had made; and he rested on the seventh day from all his work which he had made. And God blessed the seventh day, and sanctified it; because that in it he had rested from all his work which God created and made. (Genesis 2:2–3 KJV)

What a curious event that God takes leisure, contemplates, and approves of His efforts. The existence of this rest from work, which we call leisure, makes God's action of work even more vivid by contrast. Work is not only to be performed, but it is to be contemplated, evaluated, and admired. In fact, if we cannot tolerate this evaluation of work because it is uncomfortable or even painful, we end up with a distortion of leisure.

Leisure then becomes not only rest from work, but an escape from even thinking about it. This then makes leisure itself a matter of effort. As the following diagram illustrates, the high position of work and leisure descends through the Fall to become labor and mere amusement.

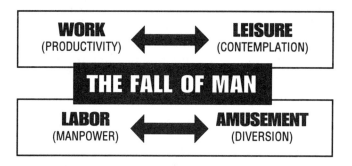

It is important to understand that the introduction of work as it appears in the book of Genesis has no connection to necessity. God did not create because He had to create, or needed to create. God has no needs or He would not be God. He is complete in Himself, and there is nothing that can be added to Him to improve Him or enhance Him or increase Him. All such ideas are absurd in view of His completeness. Since He is dynamically perfect, creation is absolutely unnecessary. It is an expression of divine exuberance.

The human version of this is seen in the highest works of human achievement, the arts referred to in previous chapters. They are of great value, not because of their material worth, but because of their significance. They express for us that which cannot be expressed in mundane discourse. They say that which otherwise could not be said about those realms of knowing and feeling in us that cannot be measured.

They are the treasures of human civilization and are of incalculable value, but they have no practical use to justify their existence. Understand art and we understand the existence of the universe. It is as marvelously purposeless as a Beethoven symphony. Similarly, it is also overwhelmingly rich with beauty and meaning. It needs no more justification than the existence of the love that gave it birth.

Unnecessary work is also seen in ordinary activities of life, where we go beyond the requirements to add the decorative, the pleasing, the interesting. We don't merely make cakes, we decorate them. We use moldings and carvings in trimming our rooms. We style our cars. We style our hair. We assemble ice cream sundaes. We landscape our property. We design unique houses. We fashion clothes for different occasions. We invent clever games to play. We grow house plants. We invent confections. We build decorative fences. We develop graphic designs. We create ambience. We assemble flower arrangements. We illustrate books. We innovate festive table settings. We make unique furniture. We play basketball. We draw doodles in our notebooks. We build fountains. We plant lawns.

If nonutility is a feature of God's work, then why can't it be the same for much of our work? I already described my work in the garden as unnecessary but satisfying. It was probably initiated by the same kind of love as was Adam's work in Eden. Adam and I enacted on a small scale what God does in measureless proportions.

Are economic reasons even close to explaining the essence of work? I suspect that if we were able to bend our ears to hear a valid reason for why God created the world, we would hear music rather than words. This lyrical idea does not mean that we reject the economic advantages of work. History shows that economic systems are repeatedly perverted by mankind on a very large scale, but they do enable us to survive. They also make it possible for us to complement one another's efforts and serve one another by producing that which we individually cannot make. The organizing and systematizing of people resources by companies and communities is a critical function to enable citizens to produce that which is useful to our well-being. Everyone benefits in this way.

But a look at the ideal might help us. Think of the value of employees in any company being so well placed that they achieve not only that which has practical, economic benefit, but also work in an arena in which they can accomplish projects they love to do and never get tired of doing. We now have the knowledge to bring this about. What blocks such progress is usually inappropriate ambition. In the new heaven and the new earth, such obstacles will cease to exist. How interesting it would be if Christian businessmen could provide a preview of how this might look.

CHAPTER TWELVE

FOCUSING A CAREER

Gaining clarity about our ambitions provides us with the overarching reason we live out our lives, especially when we introduce God into the picture. Ambition involves sweeping statements about our goals, or mission, in life. But of course we must translate this into action, which means the determination of a career. This, in turn, impels us toward certain kinds of jobs. Other than the work we do in order to survive while we are preparing for a career, the job should be the particular place in which we execute our careers. We will probably have a chain of these jobs before our lives are over.

A career can ideally be considered to be the theme of all, or most of, our jobs. It connects the different jobs we may have to the attainment of our life-goals. For the Christian, the idea of career planning involves stewardship of the gifts God has given us. We need to keep in mind not only *how* God created us (using our gifts), but also *for what* God ultimately created us. When we think in this holistic way, we can then see that it is logical and natural to connect our pleasing God to the stuff of everyday work. The following diagrams illustrate this.

Having guided thousands of individuals through the process of targeting their first career or changing careers, I recognize that most people are not well-informed about what they are doing. Students who are preparing for their first career choice usually operate under the illusion that such a decision is not especially critical. They assume that any intelligent or clever person can become whatever he decides. The factors that guide their decisions are more likely to be ones of lifestyle and money than career fit. That is one reason why the majority of students now in school are majoring in subjects that are unrelated to the careers in which they will end up.

Those involved with career change are not quite as optimistic. They have already been down the path of taking on a career that does not fit and realize they made an unhappy miscalculation. Career change is always possible and nowadays often required because of economic changes, but it is sad when an expensive education or training program turns out to have been inappropriate from the very beginning.

Without turning this into a career development manual, I would like to suggest a few steps that will enable people to make good career moves. These steps certainly should be considered before making a major investment of time and finances in a career change.

BEGIN WITH WHO YOU ARE

When Christians talk and teach about the will of God in their lives, they tend to picture it as something objective. They look for something outside themselves to guide them in the right direction. God's will is always portrayed as something to be found. It is the object of a quest.

The eagerness with which Christians are urged to find God's will is not matched by an equal degree of teaching about how that is actually accomplished. That is why, for all the talk about God's will, we find so few who convincingly claim to have found it. When we do, most often it is someone who has discovered an area of Christian ministry that happens to fit. Such people are happy to be in the position of using their God-given strengths in an activity that receives the blanket approval of both the church and the Christian culture. They feel assured that they have found God's will, when what they actually may have found is the approval of their Christian subculture. However, those who take seriously the task of being "salt" in the marketplace fare less well. Christian culture is only just beginning to affirm the value of a call to the marketplace and is somewhat reluctant to say that it is God's best will that we be there.

God's will is not a matter of something to be pursued outside ourselves. It is more a matter of discovery within. God's will is not something for which one looks any more than we should look for Abigail's will or Joe's will. Abigail and Joe do not carry their wills around in their pockets. Their wills are part of their personhood and cannot be separated from it. Similarly, God's will cannot be discovered under a toadstool or in a baptismal font. It can only be found in a relationship with God.

If you want to know my will, you will have to come into personal contact with me. If you want to know God's will, you will need to come into personal contact with Him. That, for example, was how you discovered God's intention for you to become a new creation in Christ. It came out of a personal encounter.

God's will is always active and has brought about certain results that may become signposts giving indications about some of the things He has determined. These signposts are often very helpful to us, but though they are a product of God's willful action, they should never be confused with a direct encounter with His will, which is what is necessary when we are looking for direction in our lives. A conclusion that I have strong teaching skills is a signpost. A conviction that I should take teaching job A rather than teaching job B comes out of a prayerful encounter with God's will, which is to say, God.

Very important signposts in the matter of selecting careers are the gifts He has willed into our personalities. God's definition of a person is the act of creating him. Whatever He has created us to be is the foundation with which we begin. As indicated in chapter 10, we can systematically discover the gifts we already possess in the patterns of how we went about accomplishing those achievements in which we found satisfaction. All the information with which we need to begin the process of career selection already resides within us. We must tap it.

When I do this professionally, I uncover an average of sixty to sixty-five individual unique elements of giftedness that interact with each other, so do not think for a moment that I am suggesting that you find a simplistic label for yourself. When God gives gifts, they are rich and complex and cannot be confined to the kinds of systems the world has invented. In career development, the trite procedures of the secular world are an insult to the stature of what God has created in even the most "average" person in your town.

God gives gifts and never takes them back, so though you may acquire new skills, do not expect to discover new gifts. Gifts will grow with their effective use, but they will not depart or be replaced, no more than the color of your eyes will change.

CHOOSE AN APPROPRIATE PATH

There are three paths from which to choose in response to the diversity we find in people. Each path provides a different enough perspective that the one chosen can make an important difference. However, if one path does not work well, take another for a more fitting approach. (Those who learn by experience will gladly make the necessary switch.)

PATH 1: SUBJECT MATTER

The first path is quite familiar because it is universally used in high schools and colleges. This is where individuals know they have a very strong interest in or a genius for a specific subject. Examples often line up with college course listings: physics, psychology, economics, business, finance, and medicine, for example.

One needs to determine that there has been a long-term pattern of interest in the subject matter and not a matter of novelty or of finding the subject newly interesting because of the influence of others. Students often become directed toward a misfit career because of the well-intentioned guidance of instructors who confuse outstanding academic performance in the subject they teach for potential career giftedness.

Students similarly need to analyze whether excellence in performing well in a particular subject is due to genuine in-depth interest in the subject itself or because of a motivating learning setting. A highly competitive student, for example, placed in a course in which the subject is of some interest, but where competition is key to success, would probably achieve a high grade. The high grade would be due primarily to head-to-head competition but could be misread as fascination with the subject.

Once it is clear that a particular subject is going to drive the career choice, the next step is to determine whether the interest is in applying the subject to a situation, or staying within the confines of the concepts, theory, or technology of the subject.

For example, one person may have a strong enough interest in psychology for it to be of life-long interest as a subject and could be involved with research or teaching, depending on his gifts. Another person may have an interest in psychology to provide tools or technology to enhance counseling or the teaching process. A third person may want to be directly involved with clients. He or she might counsel clients, be involved with some form of therapy program, or be a member of a professional team providing a holistic approach to clients, perhaps in a hospital setting.

The first example focuses upon *theoretical* or *conceptual* depth while the remaining two operate out of an interest in *application.* Gifts and values determine the choice and also provide the criteria for fine-tuning until a clear role is perceived.

EXAMPLE: (A simplified version of an extensive process.)

I have always had an interest in medicine and the human body, especially in how it functions.

I have always been interested in networks, connections, and systems.

I want to be involved with applications. I want to work directly with the client. I want to be in the action. I like tools and technology. I like precision. I like working with my hands. I like seeing the results of a concept.

CONCLUSION: Medicine: Neurosurgery

PATH 2: OUTSTANDING SKILL

This is where a particular skill emerges that not only is of intense interest, but where there is a high level of performance. The careers that fit this path are dependent upon a consistently increasing skill and higher levels of performance, or at least upon consistent performance. A person in this category is paid for what he can do. Examples include vocal music, instrumental music, accounting, art, dance, writing, sports, software programming, flying, acting, graphic design, and fashion design.

Many of the careers in this category involve the development of name recognition, fame, or even star quality as an intrinsic part of developing a viable career. This creates a hurdle to be overcome on the part of those who so strongly desire fame that they overestimate the level of their talent. They especially need what I recommend for everyone on this path: an assessment from at least three professionals now active in the field being considered.

No one should pursue this career path without several no-holds-barred critiques of his work or performance. Many of the career fields of this type involve a high level of competence that is always being challenged by the outstanding skills of others. A person on such a career path must have the ability to sustain these continual challenges. Once talent has been affirmed, further advice needs to be sought as to where education and training ought to take place, given the unique quality of the gift.

Having worked with professional athletes and artists in all forms of art and performance, I strongly maintain that success in these endeavors is dependent upon developing that which is true to who one is and not a duplication of someone else's style. A singer may be able to sing almost anything, but only sings certain music with excellence. A batter must find his own subtle way to achieve consistent hitting. The artist must release his own vocabulary of form and color for authentic work to emerge. In the expression of one's gift through technique, expect the unique performance to emerge from the inside out. Others can train in terms of correct methods, but they cannot impart genius. That must come from within.

PATH 3: APPROPRIATE ROLE

Seeing one's career in terms of a role is most useful where being an agent for making something happen has more meaning than thinking in terms of a subject. For example, a person who is a gifted manager may not care so much what the organization does as in having the opportunity to make a difference in helping the organization run well.

Such a manager might manage in a hospital, corporation, theater, law firm, university, retail store, airport, or town hall. In each case, the title of the position would be different, but the role would be essentially the same—working through people and systems to get results. The choice of which kind of organization would be appropriate would depend upon other factors, such as personal preference, taste, level of personal effectiveness, familiarity, or values.

This path to identifying careers is not as orderly as when one can say one is a doctor, lawyer, butcher, baker, or candlestick maker. However, its advantage is that it affords greater career flexibility in moving from one organization to another in an entirely different arena of activity, but always as a recruiter, an organizer, an administrator, a new program developer, a new program launcher, or a problem solver. It might be helpful in clarifying the role to consider whether the overarching intention in the role is

(1) to make things run smoothly, keeping the operation effective;
   or
(2) to produce changes, improving or maximizing what is already present;
   or
(3) to bring about something new in a developmental role.

YOUR PLACE

For some people, careers involve more than their work roles or profession. They need to be especially thoughtful about the place or the actual space or geography in which they work. This may incorporate anything from the specifics of the workroom they use all the way up to the town or the country in which they reside.

The Spanish language gives us the word *querencia,* which embraces the idea of being in the right place, having an affection for the place that is really home and not merely an address. The right place is the place meant for us, the place that nourishes us. It is the spot where we were meant to be, whether we were born there or searched for it or discovered it. It is the natural lair of a wild animal.

Once this place is found, one cannot casually leave it because much more would be discarded than geography. Whether surrounded by simplicity or grandeur, this place causes one's spirit to expand and grow. It teaches us the need to be good stewards of the place we are now called to be and to place great value in the eternal place to which we also have a calling. Since Jesus said, "I am going . . . to prepare a place for you" (John 14:2 NEB), we can refer to the place we have never been as even more home than our current home. The continuity of who we are now stretches from here into eternity. Do we think the One who enables us to know *querencia* would prepare an oddly foreign place? As C. S. Lewis once said, it would be strange to be hungry and there be no such thing as bread.

YOUR TIME

I am convinced that spiritual maturity has much to do with sensitivity to timing. Jesus always moved aware of the right time and in the fullness of time. His actions were orchestrated according to the nuances of what should happen and when, a matter that did not always agree with how others read circumstances. Similarly, when we engage the career development process we need to be sensitive to timing, not only on a natural basis, but more important, from a spiritual perspective. To do this, I go back to the matter of God's will being encountered in a relationship. Learning how to listen to the Holy Spirit and gaining a sense of when to move and when to be still, no matter what the signals are, is the firm ground upon which careers are built.

There is no model for you to copy in this matter. God relates to everyone differently, just as you and I relate to each of our friends in a different way. Learning when to move and when to be still will require experimentation, but be assured that God is not a reluctant participant. If you want direction, ask Him for it and be bold enough to act on what He says. Start with little items. As success reveals a pattern, increase the boldness with which you act, until you can tell the difference between your inner voice and that of God. Remember that we can never get it perfect, but perfection isn't necessary. Even the apostle Paul did not always get it right.

> But I should like you to know, my brothers, that I have often planned to come, though so far without success, in the hope of achieving something among you, as I have in other parts of the world. (Romans 1:13 NEB)

WHEN GIFTS ARE HURDLES

Gifts are intended to be a blessing, and indeed they are, because neither the world nor the church could operate without them. But we can never underestimate the human capability for botching things up. God imparts gifts to us, but we in our ignorance often misunderstand their nature, their use, and how to manage them. Because the world runs by the application of people's gifts, that misunderstanding creates all kinds of confusion and explains the zany results achieved everywhere. Sometimes greatness emerges, occasionally efficiency, but mediocrity often dominates. The fault, remember, is not the gifts, but how they are understood and applied.

Out of many possibilities, I present five families of gifts, the inherent nature of which makes those who possess them especially vulnerable to misunderstanding on the part of others, as well as themselves. Years of consulting with people about their careers and businesses have taught me that a skimpy understanding of human behavior has too often driven people to leap to conclusions that do not hold up very well. It is one thing when those decisions involve only the one making the decision, but more often than not they involve numerous employees, their jobs, and their future. The following sketches were developed to equip those for whom the commentary is appropriate, to avoid unnecessary difficulty in considering career development.

"FULFILLING REQUIREMENTS"

There are those whose gifts feature a motivated ability to respond effectively to requirements, specifications, or needs. The beauty of what they do is to provide precisely those results that have been requested, or exactly what the client needs. In most cases, they do not focus upon who they are when they are in action, but concentrate on the results. They measure their success by how well those results match what was specified.

Some of these people are leaders even though they do not look like the leadership stereotype. For example, they do not negotiate for or push their way into leadership positions but only move into position when the opportunity for leadership is either presented to them or because they are appointed. Once in a position of responsibility, and once the requirements are apparent, those who are leaders now look like leaders, some of them able to orchestrate large operations to get things done.

Since those gifted in this way are motivated by the needs of others or upon opportunities that come their way, they do not necessarily move with equal vigor when dealing with their own needs. They are pulled into the action by objective needs, not by subjective ones. In short, they cannot do for themselves what they can do so well for others unless there is a scripted process available to them for that purpose. Choosing a college major, selecting career options, and clarifying their ambitions can be a problem for them. This is especially true when we know that career development does not lend itself to tidy, orderly processes, as if life were a matter of solving geometry problems or following a script. Job-finding procedures can be organized, career processes less so. This is especially so the less the career goal is tied to an outstanding skill. Brilliant athletes, artists, or musicians have simpler decisions to make, though even in those situations they need to know where precisely they fit in their respective fields and how they should best be managed.

I recommend to clients who are motivated by requirements to explain their situation to several friends who can understand what we are presenting here. These friends can be of great value as a sounding board for ideas. They can pull together the best of the ideas into a sensible strategy and provide support while it is being carried out. What is satisfying about such support is that it doesn't involve pathology.

In doing this, requirements-gifted people need to be careful not to count on only one support person, since that individual's perspective may not be appropriate and yet could become the total strategy for action. (This can be even more of a problem if the support person is a highly respected mentor.)

A basic rule for those with requirement gifts is to consider careers where requirements or needs are naturally generated by the business process or by clients. Such settings provide the opportunity for outstanding and satisfying work. However, people with these gifts must learn to say no to that which is not appropriate for them to take on. We find in churches that people with these gifts end up doing all the volunteering, and generally are overworked.

Christians with this gift can get out of balance in their extreme attempts to fulfill all the requirements possible in their Christian faith. They more than most can come under the bondage of legalism. In that role they never feel that they have done enough. That is odd, because in their work situations the reverse happens. They invariably get a lot of credit for doing good work and staying on top of things.

Others get caught in a different trap. They become victimized by demanding leaders whose demands become requirements. When people with requirements gifts are faced with such a leader, they can be overworked and end up sacrificing family time or leisure. I have two suggestions for those of you who have any kind of fulfilling-requirements gift: keep your doctrine of justification by grace well polished and practice saying the word *no*. The world will not come to an end when you use it.

"IMPACTING" AND/OR "GAINING-A-RESPONSE"

There is a family of gifts the application of which involves making an impact upon others, be they an audience, individuals, or the world. Evangelists and actors have variations of this gift. It appears in many career fields where the persons so gifted can make their impact through whatever means their chosen field supplies.

For example, there is a difference between the lawyer who loves to solve problems for clients and the lawyer who makes the court his stage, where he makes an impression on the jury or the judge. Both kinds of lawyers have good gifts, but one cannot do best what the other is gifted to accomplish. Which lawyer should take a particular case should be determined by what the client needs.

Impacting gifts become a problem for some Christians when they consider their ambitions. It appears as if all they want is for people to pay attention or respond to them. Understandably, this seems a questionable goal to those who are concerned about their character and who cherish humility. They do not see that humility is possible in people who want to be in the spotlight, or in those who want to get a response from others. More often than not, it is assumed that individuals with such inclinations have them because they did not get enough attention during their growing-up years. This issue is too involved to discuss here except to note that while some people seek the affirmation that they did not receive as children, that does not change the fact that there are those who display strong influencing behaviors because of gifts, not pathology. Impacting and influencing gifts are evident when performance excellence indicates they are.

God cannot be pleased when those He has equipped with impacting or influencing abilities are told that their motivations are not appropriate. After all, God is the giver of the gifts. No one chooses his or her inherent gifts. God does not want the gifts withheld when they can serve others. Many people use their impacting gifts in roles as evangelists, actors, public relations professionals, and ambassadors. They honor God when they use their gifts in a manner pleasing to Him, certainly not by abandoning them.

On the other hand, wherever these gifts are present in Christian leaders, there is a tendency to assume their presence is automatically the signal of a special calling, not realizing that their secular counterparts have similar gifts that no one would label a special calling. No individual in the church should seek to secure a position in the church based on a self-proclaimed calling. The quality of his character, the depth of his walk with God, and the effectiveness of his ministry should be the evidence of how well he fits a particular position.

Humility is, for our purposes, twofold. First, it is a matter of using one's gifts appropriately, not compulsively. That is true about all gifts, including the serving, helping gifts Christian culture particularly honors. Sanctification of the gifts is what is necessary, not denial. We know sanctification has taken place when a person with specific gifts applies them where God leads him to do so, and at the right time. This is true for any gift. There are times for the evangelist to be silent. There are times for the helping and serving to cease.

Second, humility is a matter of knowing that we did not create our own gifts. We were not given the opportunity to select what we thought were the best gifts. Nor was acquiring a gift a matter of being trained to be so gifted, though we may have been trained in the skills or technology used to apply it. The reason anyone has any gift is because God gave it to him. We can take no credit for its presence. God is the only giver of gifts and will judge our faithfulness in applying them where we ought. Humility, in other words, is just a matter of admitting the facts. We cannot give a gorilla credit for being a gorilla.

"MASTERING SKILLS" AND/OR "PERFECTING RESULTS"

These gifts sometimes appear separately and sometimes together. They feature an ability to produce quality performance and/ or precise, exquisite results. Were I undergoing surgery, I certainly would prefer that the surgeon be well endowed with both gifts.

I know individuals who have gone through very trying periods of their lives with counselors they engaged to help them eliminate compulsive perfectionism. Rather than deal with the compulsive misuse of a gift, they focused upon the elimination of it. This led to the ludicrous situation where those intent on eliminating a gift were driven to do so by the very gift they sought to clobber. Imagine what the failure to do something right means to a person who wants to perfectly do something right!

The reason these gifts are presented here as a potential problem is because they can become overly active in the process of dealing with ambition and careers. As previously mentioned, career development is not a process that lends itself to a precise formula that fits everyone, nor is there an absolutely perfect result. For this reason, a principle from Augustine is appropriate: Render to each thing that degree of love it deserves. For the person who is gifted to perfect results, I modify this rule as follows: Render to each thing that degree of attention it deserves. No more and no less.

Christians with mastering skills and/or perfecting results gifts, like those who have fulfilling requirements gifts, can get trapped into rules for living the perfect Christian life and thereby miss the joys of Christian liberty. Remember that the Christian's status with God is based on the sweet experience of the unearned grace that Jesus Christ has provided. Quality achievement is a product of God's blessing, not the means to attain it.

"CONTROLLING"

Controlling gifts are another family of strengths that receive bad marks from those who only explain people in terms of pathology. Now it is true that there are individuals whose reactions to the unpredictability of life make them obsessive in their attempts to control all that possibly can be controlled. Those among this group who also have some form of controlling gifts can especially become victims of this preoccupation. However, as irritating as the tendency to control can sometimes be for those who have a relationship with, or who work with, such people, that does not justify a rejection of controlling gifts. The solution to dealing successfully with compulsive control, whatever the source of the compulsion, is to trust the love and faithfulness of Jesus Christ for one's security. That is the classic suggestion any Christian would give, and it is correct.

Discovering oneself is an organic process, not an engineering technology. When it comes to living the Christian life, those with controlling gifts need to abandon themselves to God and allow Him to unfold their lives in the sweetness of His will. They thereby learn, in ultimate terms, to trust in the One who is sovereign, rather than always depending upon their own controlling ability. In other words, they give up their idolatry.

Sharing concerns with a prayer fellowship is a great help in this process. Jesus is eager to set these gifts free to bless others. Examples of where they bless is where management of exacting results is required. Inventory control officers and air traffic controllers are a couple of striking examples where the controlling gift looks splendid as well as being a critical necessity.

"TECHNICAL FOCUS"

This label describes not merely those to whom God has given a splendid array of technical gifts, but particularly those whose gifts do not also include people as a subject matter of interest. People with a technical focus love working with technology and have no interest in working with or getting results through people. It doesn't mean they do not have friends or don't get married, because as humans they are social beings and require, as we all do, some kind of relationship with others to become healthy individuals.

Like several gifts mentioned above, this is another set of gifts that does not fit the value system of popular Christianity. It is assumed that when God converts an engineer, for example, He makes that person immediately capable of leaving engineering to get involved in ministry or missions. There is no evidence that happens. However, I do know people with technical gifts whose values also include making a difference through the impact of the Gospel. They are not preachers or teachers. They apply their technical gifts to technical responsibilities in ministry or mission organizations, easily done since contemporary missions are quite sophisticated, requiring a wide variety of capabilities.

An equally valuable option is to become a Christian presence in the marketplace, working in the technical arenas to which God has brought one. Fellow engineers will pay far more attention to what a highly competent engineer says about life than to some enthusiast they do not know. They are thereby given the opportunity to see in detail how someone walks the talk.

The love for others that God imparts to all people who come into a relationship with Him does not mean a simultaneous impartation of gifts in developing or influencing people. All of us should witness concerning the reality of God and the good news of the Gospel, wherever the Holy Spirit opens the opportunity. In the context of our work and careers, we can earn the right to be heard, and therefore we naturally exert greater influence than any outside evangelistic program. More people come to Christ under the influence of family members, relatives, friends, and fellow workers than through evangelistic programs. Finally, we should not confuse personal evangelism, which is everyone's responsibility, with strategic evangelism, which should be carried out by orchestrating the necessary variety of appropriate gifts. The first tends to be informal and proceeds from a sense of responsibility for one's fellows regardless of giftedness. The latter, being programmatic, necessitates the organized support of specialized gifts.

CHAPTER THIRTEEN
WHEN AMBITION IS DISAPPOINTED

When I look at my stature, my insignificance, and my sin, the fact that I believe I am a child of God and am, by His choice, intimately related to Jesus Christ, the Son of God, I sometimes see myself like a robin ludicrously attempting to swallow a boa constrictor instead of a worm. People who believe that sinners can become children of God must have achieved the highest plane of optimism possible.

Fortunately, those of us who do believe these facts know they are not products of exaggerated wishful thinking. We are not capable of reaching that high. God Himself had to bring us there. But in view of this admittedly rosy outlook, one would think that there might be a corresponding inability to fully appreciate the reality of suffering. The Christian must counter this reasonable conclusion with the picture of how our optimism was achieved. The good news of the Gospel was achieved through suffering. Our hopes are founded on the historical fact of an empty tomb, but it was a tomb and someone was tortured to death before being placed there.

This tempers our optimism to a profound degree. Yes, there are Christians who may embrace too much of a Pollyanna attitude, but for the most part Christians have a sober assessment of the nature of living and the possibilities of tragedy that may befall as soon as we turn any corner.

The evidence I have for this sobriety started to accumulate quite early in my life. There are several memories which haunted me for months after the events took place and which became salient visual documents of the reality of suffering. They centered around death and, at the time, they were accompanied by a feeling of seemingly indelible desolation.

In one instance, I witnessed, as a very young child, a boy younger than I thoughtlessly bolting into the street from between two cars. He was blind to the truck that crushed his skull, but I wasn't. I remember wondering if I could ever rid myself of that image and the emptiness that seemed to permeate me. Everything appeared to have slipped into slow motion. The forward leaning, scheming energy of my youthful imagination was braked, the momentum of my life temporarily halted. I had no way to obliterate what I had seen, no way to erase what had come into my mind. It haunted me for a long time.

That was the first lesson in realizing that tragedy can explode into our lives at any moment or slowly wear upon us with painful results. Later events confirmed that conclusion. One of them occurred during my teens, when split sessions at my high school had me walking lower Manhattan streets to school very early in the day. There was an appealing freshness that time in the morning in New York, which usually made the walk pleasant. But this event occurred on a frigid winter day that had me slouching deep into my jacket and muffler to escape the cold. It was also snowing, adding further discomfort. With the snow, a rare hush had come over the city.

As I trudged my way past a familiar, giant, granite building, I peered out from time to time from my nest of wool to see where I was walking. Then I saw the still figure huddled against the gray wall. He was angled against the building with his cheek against the concrete sidewalk. Flakes of snow clung to his face, softening his features, giving it a ghostly unreality. No blood. No wounds. My brain strained to comprehend what my eyes were seeing. This was death, but without the drama. No crowd. Just him and me. It was the pitiful passing of a street bum who still hugged his brown, wrapped bottle.

Before I could even consider what action I was supposed to take, I was relieved to see two men, dressed for the responsibility, swiftly approach, lift the body onto a stretcher and into some kind of van. It happened quickly. I found myself staring at the blurred sidewalk silhouette that remained. It was as if the corpse deserved no fuss on the part of his bearers and no shock on mine.

Those days we didn't have sociological labels such as street people. All I knew was that here was a classic, Salvation Army story of a man who had drunk his way into a stupor for the last time. I was old enough to know this happened, repeatedly, all over such a large city, but I didn't have to witness those deaths. Again, as with the earlier instance, I can easily recall how the bleakness of death leaked into the remainder of my school day.

This time, however, I knew more. And I was a Christian. I had ways to think about it. I was haunted by the impact of the question "What is man that thou art mindful of him?" on the statement "and not a sparrow shall fall to the ground without your Father."

I had witnessed the earthly end of a person brought into being without consultation, arbitrarily assigned a time, place, and unique complexity of physical, intellectual, and spiritual characteristics. Assigned because he obviously was not around to state his preferences. Existence was thrust on him, as on us, without access to an appeal or a legitimate escape hatch. In glad times he probably was as pleased with this arrangement as I was. Other times he, like me, just pushed on. But from time to time most of us find ourselves in the same position I was during that winter morning, trying to grasp what had taken place. *What does it mean? Is my life futile or full? How do I know?*

Though I would have preferred to avoid them, these experiences and memories have been good for me, for together with other events they have enabled my faith to be tested by the realities of life. So in the previous chapters of this book when the excitement and possibilities of knowing and investing our gifts in fitting work are portrayed, they are not done so in ignorance of those who have always struggled with careers, or those who lack the confidence to do anything this book recommends, or those whose circumstances not only force them to be in misfit situations, but to be permanently in them. There are conditions which do not, cannot, and will not change. Many people have become victims of misfortune and have railed and are still railing against its immovable presence. What is to be said about that?

I know a person who, through a childhood mishap she barely can remember, ended up with a deformed right hand. Physical therapy combined with her persistence enabled her to gain considerable use of it, yet it is a deformity she refuses to accept. She has the gifts to be out front, meeting, greeting, and negotiating with clients in the corporate scene, but she confines herself to what is for her a minor role.

Privately, she imagines herself sweeping into a conference room where important clients await. She sees herself reaching a normal right hand forward to take the extended hands of her client guests to invite them to begin exciting negotiations. That is her dream, but the part about the normal hand will never come to be.

She knows all the practical advice that any one of us would give her, but she simply will not let the preoccupation go. She stands firm in her resentment. It is almost as if she builds her identity around it. Her firm stand, however, will not do one good thing. She has imparted far more importance to her hand than it needs to bear. It is not a genuine obstacle to her dream. It is an obstacle she has unnecessarily enlarged out of a relatively small substance. Her hand will never change physically, and that is sad, but her view of it must change if she is to attain her ambitions.

Almost every individual has an inventory of changes he wishes he could bring about in his life if it were possible. There are disappointments of all kinds in most if not all of us. It may be the shape of our nose, the level of our intelligence, an inadequate work history, the character of our parents, our height, odd circumstances in our history, a disability, the emotionally crippled family in which we were reared, our looks, or a marginal education. A few of us have items on our lists that seem to justify additional complaint. They go beyond the existence of undesirable traits and include bad, or even evil, elements that have been thrust unasked into our lives and have inflicted moral or emotional damage.

However diverse these items, they have two things in common. They are empirical, factual, historical facts about us that cannot be changed. They are facts we can work around. Regardless of how painful, or bad, or weighty we find our respective burdens to be, we have the power to choose how we are going to deal with them. Some people exploit these burdens. Others transcend them. Most simply adjust in some way. Then there are those who seem determined to be inordinately absorbed with the injustice of their fate. The bad stuff of their personal histories becomes the dark glasses through which they look at all of life.

Whenever I discover this dark perspective in a person who is not a believer and who thinks that there is nothing beyond this life and its inevitable death, I can appreciate their pessimism about the present and future. It must be overwhelmingly oppressive. They place themselves in the position of assuming that the existence of evil by God's permission is so unbelievable that God cannot possibly exist. God would not let such things happen. Things ought not to be this way!

My response in those situations has been to point out the obvious. This is the way it is. They already have the evidence. Given these realities, the only alternative that makes sense to me is to believe that God must exist. Otherwise there is no possibility of restitution for unjustified wrongs, no hope that justice will be achieved, and no point to our living. Life becomes reduced to banging one's fist upon a closed door that will never open. It is the perversity of man that so many choose to cling to the bleakest conclusions and thereby become gods unto themselves. They determine their own reality which God must judge as a poisonous illusion.

There are others who respond to the grace of God and are thereby equipped to embrace hope. It is that hope that drives us toward meaningful accomplishments, because, as was described in previous chapters, such attainments can be translated into something lasting.

THE REVOLUTIONARY PERSPECTIVE

For the Christian, a preoccupation with negative conditions for which we never asked is an entirely different matter than for the unbeliever. The presence of negative conditions is what we all must expect to some degree, since we are members of a fallen race. We are sinners and the victims of sinners. But we possess this knowledge fully aware that in God's scheme of things one of the prerequisites for sainthood is to have been a sinner. Being a sinner is bad for everyone, but, fortunately, Jesus specifically ministered to the poor, the hurting, the outcast, the maimed, the disenfranchised, and the unrighteous. So when we think in kingdom terms, we know that any kind of suffering we face in life is part of the currency with which God deals.

The function of Christian hope is not to encourage us to keep a stiff upper lip or to gloss over the reality of pain. The substance of our hope equips us fully to engage life, including whatever degree of suffering is part of it. Christians assume that suffering, small or large, will pay off in terms we cannot now know, but that will ultimately amaze us. That is a major conclusion of the Scriptures.

When we see the denouement, we will agree with the conclusion that David, the sweet psalmist of Israel, made after his encounters with the injustices of life. His are remarkable verses because they do not portray the evil men who plague him as a misfortune. David chooses to believe that their unhappy presence is going to be exploited by God. He believes this so strongly that he describes his enemies as coming from God's hand!

> Keep me as the apple of the eye,
>   hide me under the shadow of thy wings,
> From the wicked that oppress me,
>   from my deadly enemies, who encompass me about. . . .
> From men which are thy hand, O Lord,
>   from men of the world, which have their portion in this life,
>   and whose belly thou fillest with thy hid treasure: . . .
> As for me, I will behold thy face in righteousness:
>   I shall be satisfied, when I awake, with thy likeness.
>   (Psalm 17:8–15 KJV; poetic form added)

How can God be so bold in His expectation that we remain faithful in the face of suffering? Because the Son of God embraced suffering to a point of extremity beyond which no one can go. We bear our own pain. He bore all pain, all suffering. For the Son of God to take on such suffering changes forever the meaning of suffering.

Prior to the Cross, suffering was restricted to being the inevitable consequence of the Fall. It was a curse. Jesus is described as One who took this curse upon Himself. He willingly took on His body and into His mind, emotions, and spirit the suffering of man. The Son of God comes from eternity outside of man's history and is therefore able to deal with all of history from its first day to the last day. This same person comes into time as a human and suffers "like passions as we" (see Hebrews 2:16 KJV; James 5:17 KJV). He owns the human experience by being a human. On the Cross He becomes a conduit that pours the power, joy, and freedom of eternity into the history of man, thereby utterly and forever changing the nature of man and his condition. Jesus assures that the experience of the Cross in history includes all the suffering that appears anywhere in history. This includes the suffering experienced by you and me, who have also appeared in history.

In the Cross and the Resurrection Jesus encounters what we perceive as the inherent absurdity of suffering to which Adam opened the door. Jesus transforms that absurdity into purpose. The empty, meaningless nature of suffering and sin ended on the day Jesus cried, "It is finished." The pain of it remains for a season of time in the same way as Christ's death remained for three days.

But all seasons end. We already know that whatever happens to us in life, when we awake from death we will be satisfied with all that God has done since the dawn of time, and especially with what He has accomplished in our individual lives. We will find no flaws.

The great Redeemer is the exploiter of wrongs, injustice, and pain to such a high degree that we know ultimately there will be no tragedy in Christ. That is why we cannot talk meaningfully and truthfully about man's lot and his suffering without understanding the Cross and the empty tomb of Jesus Christ. That is why a religion without the Cross and the Resurrection is empty, no matter how beautiful its philosophy.

Christianity is a faith that connects the glories of the Godhead to the blood, sweat, and grossness of human experience. The Cross of Jesus is the trap that conquers Satan and with him, suffering and death. The tomb of Jesus is the place where death goes in and life comes out.

The power of the Cross and the empty tomb is so extreme it shatters the ultimate disability, the terminating shame of death itself. The apostle Paul is so overwhelmed by the splendor of this victory that he ridicules death with his famous words extracted from the Old Testament: "O Death, where is your victory? O Death, where is your sting?" (1 Corinthians 15:55 NEB). Those words are now available for our lips and our lives.

WHAT TO DO

What do we do with the unchangeable negatives in our lives? The answer, in this case, is to agree with our adversary quickly. The goal is to release these negatives so they do not block our growth and progress. There are several ways Christians do this.

1. Those for whom common sense is a sufficient tool to overcome their preoccupation with their limitations practice habits of mind that refuse to cooperate with pessimism.

2. Some who discover themselves in need of spiritual support from others request such aid from their pastors and Christian communities.

3. Some are severely hampered to the point where negativism has immobilized them and they possess little strength to overcome its presence. These persons seek in-depth counseling or spiritual therapy from a community of Christians who are experienced with these matters.

Regardless of the path to healing one takes, there is a foundation that must be established to prevent any of the three approaches from becoming mere technique. We need to encounter Jesus and lay before Him all of our complaints, disappointments, suffering, history, and sin. We also need to present our gifts, joys, character, ambitions, and blessings. In other words, we must take the gift of *being* which God gave us and in its current state, regardless of the shape in which it now appears to be, present it as a gift to Jesus. It is Jesus—who suffered, bled, and died—who receives these questionable gifts from us, so that our lives will immediately come under the power of the Cross. Bringing our *being* to Him may be painful, but the Cross terminates that pain.

Later, after mourning and the inability to operate as we did in the past, resurrection takes place. We awake with the sun shining on those very things we thought intolerable to look at. We address our ambitions, realizing they now have an objective beyond those we had before, and for reasons that are not written solely in the intellect but that stir the heart. We discover that the meaning of everything has shifted. We are convinced that no matter what happens in our lives, our ambitions are attached to rich purposes in

God. We are able to engage whatever suffering becomes our lot. Even while we feel the pain, we will give it to God, assuming that He will exploit it to the hilt for ultimate glorious ends.

He does not do this to correct a mistake He has made. God cannot make mistakes. He sent Jesus as the Second Adam to correct what the first Adam unleashed upon the world. He thereby accomplishes that which could not otherwise be accomplished. He brings the will of man to its greatest power. Though the will of Adam and Eve was great enough to retain or reject paradise, it had no power to change their positions in the hierarchy above them. God was and always will be highest. Below God was the domain of angels, and below them came man. The occupants of all three levels communicated with each other with great clarity. Then, by their own choice and by the power of the will God gave them, Adam and Eve lost their place in the hierarchy. Communication between them and God was shut down.

What was God's response? God, in His love, initiated new communication through selected prophets. That is the story of the Old Testament. The prophets spoke for God to His people and spoke of days to come and a future Suffering Servant, who would replace both priest and prophet. These prophecies prepared the way for God to communicate to fallen humankind in the most direct way possible, and that is through His Son. He sent Jesus, who mediated the great restoration. But mankind was not restored to Eden. Nor did Jesus move us higher to have equality with angels. Instead, He accomplishes the unbelievable. He announces that we can be one with Him in the family of God. We have the potential of being swept above Eden, above the hierarchies of angels, and into intimacy with God. Once again man is given the opportunity to choose.

The choice is as extreme as it can be. The alternatives are as far as the east is from the west. The objects of choice are oneself or God. To choose oneself is to retain disease and suffering and to fasten ambition on goals that will turn to dust. To choose God is to gain that for which we were made. It is to be lifted higher than the angels into God Himself. That is a glorious destiny beyond our complete comprehension, but is nevertheless revealed by Jesus. All the grandeur of the earth and the universe become pictures of that potential glory.

In contrast, when we look at the history of mankind choosing itself, we find everything from trouble in families to extremities of horror in societies. These troubles signal the absurdity of choosing ourselves over God. Such lessons of history should drive us in panic to God, lest we once again lose our opportunity to be set free from the curse mankind brings upon itself.

IDENTIFYING FREEDOM

Given the truth of what Jesus has done for us, we know it is possible to achieve genuine freedom from the intimidation of our negative history, limitations, and weaknesses. With the Holy Spirit's empowerment, we can boldly take on whatever is necessary to bring that freedom into the practical areas of our work and relationships. We can expect that God will support us as we turn from our compulsive preoccupation with ourselves to make a difference to others.

We can leave the safety of our churches and plant ourselves as living testimonies in the marketplace, the corporation, the courts, the universities, the high schools, and the banks; on the farms; in the Congress and in the town halls; in grocery stores, insurance agencies, hospitals, shops, laboratories, utilities, and manufacturing plants as mediators of God's love, power, grace, and healing.

The tempter will come to recite a litany of negatives aimed at reminding us that, given our past, we have no right to speak to the marketplace. We may agree with the facts of whatever he says, but not his conclusions. We have no reason to care about what he thinks. Our attitude thereby forces everything into a new perspective that does not change the facts, but radically changes what those facts mean.

None of us can pretend we are not sinners. However, what that used to mean is quite different from what it now means this side of God's grace. Similarly, the bad things that infected our lives are historical facts. They did happen to us. We were actors or victims in those events, but we do not intend to stay there. We starve any resentment that emerges as soon as it rears its ugly head until it wastes away. We become careless about our past and pursue the hope of our high calling.

[A good man] will not be afraid of evil tidings; for his heart is steadfast, trusting in the Lord. (Psalm 112:7 NKJV)

It is sad to discover mature adults who have heard this good news but are still devoted to repeatedly reviewing life's disappointments. Instead of engaging the ambition God has given to accomplish something of value, they are still going over the same old stories and justifications for not taking action. That is their decision. They do not have to remain in their misery even when they are powerless to get out by themselves. God is always available to them. They can respond to His daily invitation to be objects of his lavish love. They can embrace the sheer optimism of the apostle Paul, who surely had things of which he could complain.

God knew his own before they ever were, and also ordained that they should be shaped to the likeness of his Son, that he might be the eldest among a large family of brothers; and it is these, so foreordained, whom he has also called. And those whom he called he has justified, and those whom he justified he has also given his splendour. . . .

[God] did not spare his own Son, but gave him up for us all; and with this gift how can he fail to lavish upon us all he has to give? . . . What can separate us from the love of Christ? Can affliction or hardship? Can persecution, hunger, nakedness, peril, or the sword? . . . For I am convinced that there is nothing in death or life, in the realm of spirits or superhuman powers, in the world as it is or the world as it shall be, in the forces of the universe, in heights or depths—nothing in all creation that can separate us from the love of God in Christ Jesus our Lord. (Romans 8:29–39 NEB)

Although this book urges the pursuit of goals that are appropriate for our values and our gifts, there are times when we are prevented from pursuing the very thing for which we were made. My father experienced the deprivations of the Great Depression at a point in his life when he was getting close to the position that fit his interests. Those for whom he worked lost most of their fortune as a result of the Stock Market crash, which, in turn, required the termination of my father's services.

At that point, he had a family totally dependent upon him. Years later, when I asked him how it was to go through those difficult years, he told me that there was no time when God was not faithful to supply all our needs as a family. God never failed him. Justified complaint ("Why was I not brought into a more opportune situation?") was ignored by him. The last photograph we have of him expressed this disregard for the negatives of his life. It was taken on the day he died. I see it now across the room as I write. His face is turned toward the camera. He is beaming. That smile deprived self-pity and self-centered attitudes of even a fragment of significance.

I wonder what we would discover if we were able to compare those tough Depression years to the more successful times of my father's life. Is there not a possibility that something of dazzling value will be seen in my father's character when I encounter him again in eternity, something that emerged out of his most difficult years in providing for his family, in providing for me? I am convinced that is true. I am convinced because those are the uncompromising terms of God's grace as revealed to each of us by the Holy Spirit. If we let Him, God will relentlessly squeeze the hardships of our lives until they produce that which is of inestimable value and glory.

PART FOUR
GOD IS OUR DESTINY

Who do you say that I am?

CHAPTER FOURTEEN

THE GOLDEN BOY

Our future is not a matter that we can leave to the future if we expect it to be hopeful. The Bible states inflexibly, "The fool has said in his heart, 'There is no God'" (Psalm 14:1 NASB). It is hazardous to maintain a shallow idea of God, because that shallowness will affect our perception of our earthly and heavenly destinies. We will have no power whatsoever to change our ultimate destiny when we are in it. Our future status is determined by each individual as he or she goes through the process of time. It is obvious to all of humankind that this process will inevitably come to an end. The Bible proposes that we make this end a grand entrance.

But an entrance into what? That has been determined by the work of God. If we have made Him into someone He isn't, we will get uneasy about our future with and in God. If we know God in terms of who He reveals Himself to be, then the results will inevitably be winsome.

This section of the book deals with the distinctives of God and of each of us, and it discusses the unique relationship each of us has with God. The book ends with comments on how the distinctives of persons and of God affect our roles in a competitive and insecure world.

THE GOLDEN BOY

The Golden Boy is the exemplar, the Superman. He appears in one form or another in the stories, fables, myths, and songs of humanity going back into ancient times. In history, he is Alexander the Great. In fairy tales, he is the prince. In fables, he is King Arthur with his Knights of the Round Table. In high school and college, he is the football star who is also the honors student, class president, and the one voted most likely to succeed.

Regardless of the century in which they live, the Golden Boys share common features. They look right and act right—to such a degree that they irritate those of us who are not so gilded. No wonder they attract injustice like honey does a bee, but even there they somehow emerge unscathed.

A biblical example of the Golden Boy is seen in Joseph, whose story is found in the book of Genesis. Joseph is a model of the person who does everything right and a preeminent example of success.

> Joseph had a dream; and when he told it to his brothers, they hated him still more. He said to them, 'Listen to this dream I have had. We were in the field binding sheaves, and my sheaf rose on end and stood upright, and your sheaves gathered round and bowed low before my sheaf.' His brothers answered him, 'Do you think you will one day be a king and lord it over us?' and they hated him still more because of his dreams and what he said. (Genesis 37:5–9 NEB)

Now Joseph did not have to tell his brothers his dream, nor the similar one that followed, but he did, and it isn't difficult for us to imagine the smugness in his demeanor as he did so. Without approving of his brothers' crimes against Joseph, we can understand why they resented him: Joseph was so very, very good and did everything right. More than that, he ended up in Egypt second only to Pharaoh in authority. In that position he played coy games with his brothers that dramatized his persona, much the same way his dreams did.

My version of the story of Joseph incorporates a sour grapes attitude, and that is significant. As I was growing up, I developed an attitude toward God based on an image of a human being who does everything perfectly. I knew that God's righteousness went beyond that of Joseph. God was the absolutely good person. I was supposed to love Him, and the reality of an early conversion experience made my love genuine.

This love was tainted by a hidden irritation over the fact that God was always right—and clearly I was not. His unflawed state and unlimited power did not sit well with me, though I could not directly admit such a thought, so I suspect it ended up as an attitude. Given what I have written in the preceding chapters about God, it is clear that radical changes took place in my thinking over the years, but as a youngster I found that it was hard to think of God without some element of fear being present.

I knew instinctively that it was absurd for me to critique God. I wasn't ignorant. I knew that the very definition of God could not include anything less than perfection. The problem was that I didn't think perfection was entirely attractive. I thought it too predictable. It also bothered me that God, like Joseph, appeared to take pleasure in the idea that others should bow before Him. God seemed to me to have an inordinate interest in receiving obeisance and praise. Certainly, God's demand that He alone be praised occurs throughout the Bible, often backed up with threats, as though He were a parent making a child say "Thank you" whether or not the child actually felt gratitude.

As a boy I could understand my parents teaching the grace of good manners, but I could not understand being required to feign an attitude that was not genuine. It was irksome that I would be commanded to be thankful for something that I might not actually appreciate. It was additionally irritating that my parents would usually got the response they wanted. They backed up their expectations with parental authority. Parental threats, however, were mild in comparison to the chilling portents pronounced by God to coerce desired behavior. Here is an example announced to the nation of Israel, by God's spokesman Jeremiah.

> Give glory to the Lord your God, before he cause darkness, and before your feet stumble upon the dark mountains, and, while ye look for light, he turn it into the shadow of death, and make it gross darkness. (Jeremiah 13:16 KJV)

Apparently God not only demands that His people give Him glory, but comes close to forcing them to do it. Given God's insistence that we give Him praise in spite of how we might feel, it isn't odd that some people wonder if it would really be utter delight to spend eternity with such a being. How many Hallelujah choruses are we capable of singing? It is one thing to have a third party, such as David, prompting us to praise God, but it is another to have the One who is the object of praise give the order for its delivery.

The secular world at times makes allowance for religious people who have a fear of God. The world fears anyone who carries a big stick. An intelligent individual would want to be on the good side of such a divinity. That makes common sense. Many nonbelievers think that formal worship is to be expected of religious people. To them it is like saying "Yes, Boss" to a Mafia kingpin. They too would be saying "Yes, Boss" to God, if they thought for a moment that He existed and couldn't be avoided. What much of the world cannot understand is why people should be genuinely enthusiastic about God.

GRATITUDE

The usual reason given for the need for Christians to praise God is gratitude. This idea fills book after book and sermon after sermon. Though at times the subject can become tedious by the force of repetition, all Christians believe that thankfulness is appropriate in light of what God has done with the sin that corrupts men's lives. Not only has God dealt with the guilt of sin's existence, but also He has dealt with the inner source of its production. Freedom from the inherent sickness of the soul triggers springs of gratitude within the soul that naturally demand expression.

That is why church buildings of all kinds—storefronts, pavilions, tents, meeting houses, tabernacles, and cathedrals—have reverberated with the sounds of thanksgiving ever since the day of Pentecost. Splendid varieties of sound—robust shouts, hand-clapping choirs, roaring organs, singing congregations, and orchestras of all kinds—have poured out everything from gospel songs, hymns, and anthems to ethereal ancient chants. All of it is felicitous, for throughout history the people to whom God has given extraordinary liberty and joy gather in those places of worship.

To these celebrations of Christians should be added the persistent praises of faithful Jews ever since Abraham was called to the land of Canaan, extending through the centuries and lasting to this day despite the Diaspora and more than one holocaust. The Jews praise God because they were called to be His people. Though they argue from time to time about the advantage of such a designation, and though God has for them been silent since the day the temple in Jerusalem was destroyed, somehow they still know that God is not through with them. I believe that is true, and I am full of gratitude for their centuries of testimony about the God of Abraham, Isaac, and Jacob. The Jews provided the culture and the bloodline out of which our Savior was conceived and nurtured.

Deserved gratitude explains why we should praise God, but it does not explain the word *glory* in the verses quoted from Jeremiah. David, of the Old Testament, refers to the King of glory (Psalm 24:7), which portrays more than divine authority and capability, but a presence permeated by splendor. If the all-powerful God can be said to carry anything, it is not a big stick, but a scepter. The first is a symbol of brute power; the second a signal of inherent authority. The scepter does not back up authority. It signals that He is ultimate authority. Unlike the big stick, the scepter is beautiful.

This is the point of God's glory; it is the radiance of His stunning presence. He is the glorious King of Glory. He not only generates all genuine glory but is in Himself unimaginable, glorious beauty, beauty behind all other beauty. The glory of the Father and the Son and the Holy Spirit was self-witnessed within the mystery of the prepotent Trinity before mankind was on the scene to perceive it. God's radiance has always been. Humanity merely adds to that music.

THE POND

The morning I began this chapter, I took a walk and observed the dance of nature above and below the glimmering surface of a pond. I was familiar with most of the birds, insects, fish, and amphibians that flicked, flew, and swam before my eyes. I was also aware of the microscopic life that supported much of the visible life I saw before me. In addition, I knew the facts of the overwhelmingly complex, interrelated systems that held it all together.

But this morning something broke through those layers of facts and familiarity. Sensation and knowledge coalesced into the realization of intense beauty. I returned to the house knowing that I had had an encounter with a splendor sometimes hidden and sometimes apparent in the display of nature. I saw something of glory, and it was wonderful in itself, not just as an agent of some other purpose.

I cannot perceive the glory of beauty merely by looking at nature. There are times when what I saw that morning appears solely as phenomena. I may know it as beautiful phenomena, but that differs from the experience of beauty. The sensations I experienced at the pond triggered some capacity within me that released the glory of the moment. Time and again, throughout my life, certain sensations have brought about a similar experience. One cannot anticipate what music—or landscape, or face, or story, or words, or nostalgia, or event—will open the door to glory, or the longing for glory. Glory bursts in unexpectedly but is no less welcome for its spontaneity.

If we trace any encounter with glory to its ultimate source, we will always end up with God. The beauty of any natural object is that which God created. The beauty of the child is only possible because He made it so. The beauty of music and poetry and stories could not exist without God's giving mankind the gifts to originate them. Ultimately, all perceived glory can only emanate from God's glory, and His glory is one with His staggering beauty. To know God is to know both.

Why does God demand that we give Him praise, that we pay attention to Him? Why does He keep interfering with our self-sufficiency and independence? Why cannot a person work out a truce with God, an agreement that He should let us be and we will let Him be? If such an idea made any sense at all and could possibly be arranged, the signature on that contract would be a death sentence. The demand for independence is a juvenile, illusionary desire in the lives of millions. People want to be left alone, but God repeatedly proclaims throughout the ages of history that He is the only One who can make people complete and fully human and satisfy the longings that have preoccupied them all their lives. People want to be left alone, but they cannot be left alone and remain human. There is no compromise possible in this matter. No halfway measure exists. There is no third, less demanding option. It is either all or nothing.

It all ends in God because there is no place He cannot be. We came from God, and we will all return to Him and must find that to be either intolerable pain or concentrated bliss. God is heaven for those who love Him and hell for those who do not. Those who love Him are always moving closer to Him, even in these present moments. Those who declare God the enemy are moving swiftly away from a God from whom there is no "away." The friction of this un-ending escape generates the heat of their agony. They were not made for themselves, so God asks again what He once asked the Israelites ages ago: "Why, O why will you die?" (see Ezekiel 33:11).

Can we find bliss with God? Not if we see him as a Golden Boy, or as a demanding divinity who needs us to bow before Him repeated-ly, or as One who can always shake His rockets and win, or as an eternal cop in the sky, or any other false image we have developed in our minds. If He is any of those things, we would vote for another divinity. And God would agree with the vote. He knows that every one of those images of Him is an idol—and we already know God's opin-ion about idols. When people register their dissatisfaction with false gods, they are using a standard of judgment that comes from God.

From what source do we think the ability to tell what is or is not appropriate for God came? If any person has an aversion to boredom, it is because God gave it to him. How else would the One who is the source of life feel about boredom? If anyone has a truth-ful view of divinity, it is because God provided it.

It was God who made it possible for me as a boy to realize that He isn't a monumentalized Golden Boy. He is not a god who has decided to be good. He is the divine Judge who defines what good is by nature. He can do that because He is beyond good. He is holy. The god who is desperate for attention is no God.

Worship is for our sake, not His. We know that His power can-not be described in Department of Defense images because God's power is behind all power that is. Every legitimate longing we ever had can only be satisfied in Him. More than that, they are *ultimately* satisfied in Him. The deep capacities for delight and pleasure we know as part of finite existence are but hints of the indescribable bliss that is unavoidable in the presence of the One who invented pleasure, because He is in Himself ultimate pleasure.

I was once asked to be the speaker for the ten-minute chil-dren's sermon that was occasionally part of the Sunday morning worship in our church. I wanted to talk to the children about God. I felt a need to furnish a simple word that would help them escape the usual ideas that keep God boxed away in the Sunday school department of their minds. Happily, the theological omni-words conventionally used for the attributes of God were too far above the heads of these children for me to use. I looked instead to what about God attracts me and has always been true for me: God is interesting. In fact, He is very interesting!

After pointing out a number of natural objects to the children that they all agreed were fascinating, I asked how they come to be so interesting. With some guidance, they developed good theology by concluding that the things we looked at were interesting because God made them, and He had to be far more interesting than anything He made.

They ended with the happy, simple, true conclusion: They were in the care of a heavenly Father who will always be very, very interesting. That insight will help them when church is interesting. They will know why. It will also help them when church is boring. They will know why.

HEAVEN

If God is interesting, what is heaven like? The best way to answer that question is by asking another question. What kind of heaven would be created by the inventor of chimpanzees, mountains, honey, flowers, coffee beans, Sequoia evergreens, dolphins, trout streams, mushrooms, turtles, emeralds, rice, grass, autumn, the scent of a campfire, the scent of Lily of the Valley, frost crystals, dogs, roses, music, swallows, asparagus, horses, chipmunks, willows, apples, raspberries, brooks, beaches, butterfly fish, lobsters, electricity, forests, falcons, sex, lemons, beetles, broccoli, and oceans? Surely a heaven designed by such an extraordinary designer would have to be an extraordinarily astonishing place.

We must add to the delights of heaven the fact that its citizens will dwell there forever and will see and know its King. All the fair beauties and handsome faces found on earth have little prepared us for the ultimate beauty of our King. What will it be like, when we have done all and placed our works at His feet? What will it be like to see Him turn His face upon us and say, "Well done, thou good and faithful servant: thou hast been faithful over a few things, I will make thee ruler over many things: enter thou into the joy of thy lord" (Matthew 25:21, 23 KJV). It sounds like more work. Now that will be very, very interesting.

> Eye hath not seen, nor ear heard, neither have entered into the heart of man, the things which God hath prepared for them that love him. (1 Corinthians 2:9 KJV)

CHAPTER FIFTEEN

DISTINCTIVENESS

There is a quality about God that is quite conspicuous, and that is His love of distinctiveness. We do not have to go through any theological or academic doors to perceive this, because we swim in it. Sky is distinct from land, up is distinct from down, black is distinct from white, birds are distinct from snakes, abstract is distinct from concrete, you are distinct from me, and we are distinct from God. Even within the oneness of God Himself there are the distinctives of the Trinity. This is so readily perceived that it in some way seems peculiar to refer to it, but I do so because the obvious display of distinctiveness surrounding us has not reduced our human tendency to cultivate uniformity and conformity. It is not unusual for leaders to challenge us to copy the ideals and actions of contemporary stars or historical heroes. We are repeatedly expected to modify our behavior so that it duplicates someone else's. There does not seem to be equal interest in affirming our distinctiveness.

In the Christian context, I think it is a fine idea to tell the stories of our spiritual heroes. I can never read the impassioned review of the faithful portrayed in the eleventh chapter of Hebrews without being energized anew about my faith. It is a rousing passage. The author undoubtedly intended for it to be so in order to spur us on to run successfully our own "race that is set before us." In the contemporary setting, however, we get the feeling that we never achieve enough. As a result, many Christians assume that if they were to receive grades for how they live their lives as do students for their work, they would be earning low to average marks or less. We are expected to do more, and quite often we are expected to do it in a particular way for the results to be acceptable. It is as if God were a drill sergeant taking us through our routines, and we never manage to deliver the precision and the spit and polish He expects of us.

This inclination toward conforming effort is more pronounced in some Christian communities than others, but it appears as a characteristic of Christian culture as described in chapter 7. It locks us into a prison cell of religious effort in which our achievements become proof of our commitment rather than expressions of our love and service. Though that is a matter of poor biblical theology, that is not the point I wish to make here. The problem I am addressing is the standard-setting mentality that accompanies these urges toward excellence Most of us applaud the desire for excellence, but the Scriptures do not give us reason to believe it can be successfully achieved by always copying standards external to ourselves. We have been warned about this in the Scriptures.

> Each man should examine his own conduct for himself; then he can measure his achievement by comparing himself with himself and not with anyone else. For everyone has his own proper burden to bear. (Galatians 6:3–5 NEB)

The last phrase of this reference presents the idea that we are unique to such a degree that the burdens and responsibilities each of us carries differ from those of everyone else. As individuals, we gain from God those responses that are appropriate to who we are. Similarly, we should not treat others as though they are not also unique, nor should we evaluate their varied successes against the standard of our performance. Consider the admonition given by the apostle Paul about the unique faith each of us possesses by God's grace.

> Do not be conceited or think too highly of yourself; but think your way to a sober estimate based on the measure of faith that God has

dealt to each of you. For just as in a single human body there are many limbs and organs, all with different functions, so all of us, united with Christ, form one body, serving individually as limbs and organs to one another.

The gifts we possess differ as they are allotted to us by God's grace, and must be exercised accordingly. (Romans 12:3–6 NEB)

Thinking our way to a "sober estimate" should be based on what God has given us, not on what other people expect. Now there are plenty of standards portrayed in the Scriptures, but they are usually moral standards that apply to everyone. No Christian, for example, should cheat anyone at any time. Moral qualities are similar in all Christians if we compare one Christian to another, but behavior that is triggered by our gifts is distinctive by nature. God wants us to know this so that we can be wise in choosing where to apply our gifts as an expression of our faith in Him. That is what "sober estimate" means. Notice that in the Scripture passage, faith and gifts are concordant. They work together.

Our spiritual growth requires that we increasingly express in action what God peculiarly made us to be. As we do so, we advance in our understanding of how God has equipped us and where He wants that equipment used. This does not always happen. There are scores of Christians who are at this moment pursuing careers as accountants for the simple reason that they believe that there will be jobs for them when they graduate. They have never asked whether their gifts fit such a career nor whether they can serve best in that capacity. They have never asked whether God is honored by their choice, because they do not know their own uniqueness, nor have they been taught how to please their Creator by being what He made them to be. They are pursuing goals that are convenient or safe rather than those that are in harmony with who they are. When they graduate and get into accounting jobs, unless accounting actually fits their gifts, they are not likely in their work to develop self-knowledge and the confidence that should accompany it. Yet it is critical to our well-being that we gain the confidence found in our kinship with Jesus Christ. That will permit us to move from the secure center of our faith to its perimeter, where faith encounters doubt. That is the precise point where we grow in our faith. Spiritual advance involves victorious invasions into territories over which the flag of doubt flies. They are conquered and then included in the arena of faith.

If God has given us a large measure of faith, then we can expect extensive expansion of kingdom domain. If God has given a small measure of faith, then we expect its equal in expansion because the perimeter of faith is smaller. In this case, large or small is irrelevant to God. Faithfulness is the key issue. We should execute the advance of which we are capable, given the level of faith we have been given and have cultivated. In one situation that means the courage to leave a misfit job to take on one that fits. In another it means trusting that God will supply the financial resources we otherwise do not have to accomplish what He has called us to do. In still another, it means confronting any corporate culture that places profits before honesty. In another situation it means helping someone through difficult circumstances, though the obstacles seem to be insurmountable.

This kind of spiritual expansion does not emerge out of spiritual timidity or conformity to religious conventions. We must be strong, and sometimes daring. But when we work in misfit jobs, we tend not to have the energy or the confidence that would enable us to take on the battles of life with rigor. In fact, misfit situations sap our strength. When we work where we belong and pour energy into tasks that motivate us, somehow, in God's economy, we get energy back. To him who has, more is given.

RELATING TO GOD

It is no secret that such vitality does not come through simple awareness of the truth, although that is a great blessing. It comes out of a dynamic relationship with Jesus, who is the truth. It is established by listening to, talking with, and listening to God again and again, day by day, event by event, communicating what we think and how we feel, requesting His help, addressing our troubles, and appreciating His love. He has comprehensive knowledge of us, so the purpose of our prayer is not to be informative. Prayer functions in several ways.

1. Prayer enables us to confess the realities of our state to the One who can transform them. Our experience of reality must be improved when we encounter ultimate reality.

2. Through prayer, we are given the power to reverse unfavorable situations in which we find others or in which we find ourselves.

3. Through prayer, we enhance our sensitivity to the need for appropriate action and pick up the signals of where and when to take it.

4. In prayer, we express our love and gratitude and tap the spiritual depths for which we were made.

All of the above equips us to focus upon our next venture. In the beginning, as we listen, the voice of the Holy Spirit will sound like ours, but nevertheless we can act on what we hear. We begin with small obediences until we are capable of hearing more of the Holy Spirit's accent than ours. We can enjoy His presence and hear His love for us rather than merely acknowledge His love. We can begin to realize that each of us knows God in a way no other person can.

The Scriptures display that every relationship between God and any person is distinctive. Each person is equipped by his or her gifts to *see* and appreciate a particular aspect of God that no one else can quite perceive in the same way. Each person can thereby *celebrate* an aspect of God no one else can. King David, for example, knew that he had the gifts of a warrior. He was also a poet. In the unusual role of poet/warrior he describes God frequently in military terms as the One who vanquishes His enemies. David communicates with God in a way that is very unlike the way I communicate with Him.

> [God] is the shield of all who take refuge in him.
> What god is there but the Lord?
> What rock but our God?—
> the God who girds me with strength
> and makes my way blameless,
> who makes me swift as a hind
> and sets me secure on the mountains;
> who trains my hands for battle,
> and my arms aim an arrow tipped with bronze.
> (Psalm 18:30–34 NEB)

David contrasts strongly with someone like Ezekiel, with his bizarre behavior, or the winsome Ruth, from the book of the same name, who is characterized by faithful love. Each of them had their own unduplicated relationship with God. Each saw in Him aspects others could not discern. They have enriched my understanding of God as I see the contrasts between them and how God responded to each in the stories of their lives.

In the unhurried world of divine creation, God precisely devised a particular genius in each of us. Within our bodies He inserted those physical and intellectual capabilities necessary to carry out and express our singular nature. Bringing forth this uniqueness should characterize all careers, all worship, and all relationships, so that each of us displays the distinctiveness God loves. Since each human personality is different, every human relationship is different. Those differences are not mild. They are very strong. We even relate differently to each of our friends, all of whom may be on an equal footing with us.

What is true between us and human personalities is also true of our relationship with God. Every relationship with God is different. Even the way each of us hears from God is unique, as is also the path on which He takes us in life. Given the temper of Christian culture, where leaders are prone to make principles for others out of the way God happened to guide them, it is necessary for each of us to realize the authenticity of his own connection with God. He knows our uniqueness and relates to us accordingly. Others cannot have as comprehensive an understanding of us as our designer; therefore, their models often impose upon us that which is not appropriate. Erasmus once said, "It is the chiefest point of happiness that a man is willing to be what he is." This is a charming but pointed way of recognizing that we should obey the will of God revealed in how He created us. Of all the creatures on the planet, and perhaps in the universe, what a personal honor there is in carrying the thumbprint of God upon our being! This is the foundation for self-confidence. Herein is the suitable trigger for our ambitions. Forget the reluctant accolades of our contemporaries. Consider what it means to have the loving approval of the King of all that is.

AFFIRMATION

For the individual and the community, any attempt to know and understand ourselves outside the context of God is a fruitless occupation. We have already seen in Scripture that any attempt to determine our own value by comparing ourselves to others is also meaningless, because we do not know what God is doing in the lives of those whom we would use as a standard. Some of our fellow believers achieve feats that surpass our own. They ought to surpass us because of the large measure of faith they have been given. Much will be expected of those to whom much has been given (see Luke 12:42–48). The particular level of a person's gifts has little to do with the quality of his character. Someone may or may not be splendid in spiritual qualities, but we have few ways of knowing, nor is that knowledge usually of any importance to us except when it is a matter of leadership selection. It is much like attempting to judge who actually contributed the most when the collection basket came around. Look at how Jesus evaluates the widow's contribution in the gospel of Luke.

> [Jesus] looked up and saw the rich putting their gifts into the treasury; and he saw a poor widow put in two copper coins. And he said, "Truly I tell you, this poor widow has put in more than all of them; for they all contributed out of their abundance, but she out of her poverty put in all the living that she had." (Luke 21:1–4 RSV)

None of this proposes that we can live without knowing that our contributions are worthwhile. Nor does it suggest that Christians do not need affirmation. God designed us with a capacity for recognition. That is why we have names. He made us to be objects of approval and blessing, which is why these matters are so important to us. The need is there because, as social beings, we are made to give and receive honor. Approval should begin very early in our lives in order for us to develop self-confidence. We need to receive enthusiastic accolades from our families, who, we hope, love us for who we are in ourselves and who can be somewhat careless about what we achieve. Inside and outside the family, we should be especially generous in our affirmation of each other. It is abnormal for a society not to let its members know their value. When families and communities are incapable of providing appropriate expressions of affirmation, they drive individuals to satisfy that need in inappropriate ways that are destructive of both the individual and society.

WHEN AFFIRMATION IS SPARSE

As Christians, we can have a relationship with God that enables us to function even in times of sparse appreciation for our contributions. When we know God's eye is upon our work, not in a spirit of accountability but in a spirit of love, we can be less affected by the temperamental nature of people around us. God's love toward us is specific, not generalized, as is to be expected of the One who invented the individual. Aside from giving us the joy of being the object of His love, God's delight in us has its practical function. It sets us free to be bold in pursuing those ambitions that fit us. We can remain constant, even though our goals may not fit what our culture or our friends expect or want us to be. We will then be individually empowered and equipped to take our place in the marketplace, expecting to make a difference. We can cultivate the presence of God wherever we are because He has made Himself available to us wherever we are. Here are some steps which may be helpful to some readers in discerning this intimate, distinctive relationship with God.

WHAT TO DO (IF IT FITS YOU)

1. *Think about, or think and write about, those times in the past where God spoke to you, nudged you, convicted you, arranged circumstances, directed you, delighted you, or guided you.* When you have enough items to do so, look for a pattern in how God relates to you. If you see a pattern, articulate a statement that characterizes the particular way God relates to you. If you keep a spiritual journal, repeat this exercise from time to time to see how your statement should be expanded as you discover and learn more about yourself and God. If it is difficult for you to remember the past or to perceive consistencies, ask the Holy Spirit to open your memory and to guide your mind. Be careful that you don't try to make the evidence fit some ideal you already have in your head. Let the evidence grow on its own.

Some individuals find a consistent pattern in how God speaks to them. Others are like the apostle Paul, who at one time hears a voice calling him to Macedonia, another time has a conviction, and still another is given a clear word from the Lord. Despite the variety, the apostle Paul knew, probably with few exceptions, when God was speaking to him. There was an internal signal consistent enough for the apostle Paul to conclude when God was or was not speaking. Compare two of statements in 1 Corinthians (7:10, 12 NEB):

> I give this ruling, which is not mine but the Lord's . . .

> To the rest I say this, as my own word, not as the Lord's . . .

We know that as an apostle Paul could be expected to receive an extraordinary degree of clarity from God, especially since much of what he understood became inspired Scripture. However, though what God communicates to us now is not going to end up as Scripture, we are taught by the New Testament that each of us can grow in the knowledge of God and in knowing His will.

> If any of you falls short in wisdom, he should ask God for it and it will be given him, for God is a generous giver who neither refuses nor reproaches anyone. (James 1:5 NEB)

2. *From time to time in your Bible study, focus upon a particular character who interests you.* See if you can determine something about how God uniquely communicated and involved Himself with that person. Be careful to perceive what the Scriptures portray and not impose a predetermined conclusion. Is it true that God has a fresh approach to each person?

3. *Review the information you have developed in steps 1 and 2.* What patterns do you see that could guide you in perceiving when God is communicating with you or guiding you? Given the evidence you have, what is the best way for you to seek God's direction or involvement? What setting enhances your discovery of God talking to you? How would you best sensitize yourself to His voice?

4. *Once you have determined that God has given you direction, if it is appropriate, share it with others you trust to get their wisdom.* Then take action. Do what you believe you are supposed to do and evaluate the results. Can you now conclude that God actually directed you? If so, express your appreciation to Him for that guidance and take the next step. Keep repeating the process, but in the beginning only in situations in which a mistake is not going to be a serious problem. Start with small things and gradually work

your way up to big ones. With each step of obedience you will gain increased trust for the next step, and so it will go until you can take on large and important steps of faith with increased confidence in God. At no time will you be immune from error. Humans are fallible. What will happen is that you will develop a particular style of communicating with God which fits the measure of faith God has given you. Never make this a norm for anyone else. You can tell your story of God's guidance while encouraging others to develop their own relationship with Him. You can encourage them and pray with them, but you cannot make them a clone of you.

5. *Review the passages in this book that describe God. What are the implications of what has been written?* What statements about God attract you? As you read your Bible, what do you find appealing in its descriptions of God and how He acts? What about God makes you uneasy? Keep a list of the aspects of God's personality you especially find interesting. When you have enough items on your list, analyze it. Do you see any aspects of God's personality, as you perceive Him, that are especially winsome to you? Is there any connection between what you know about your gifts and the qualities about God that intrigue you?

6. *Develop a language of prayer and praise out of your list from step 4.* Read some of the psalms of David and consider how his character is revealed in his writing. Think about the quality of words as words and how they have been used by God and His saints to express the grand stories and teachings of the Bible. Consider how to express yourself to God in words that are both rich in meaning and particularly expressive for you.

I sometimes incorporate verses from old hymns for my private devotions. They have the advantage of always focusing upon God, in contrast to modern lyrics, which tend to concentrate mostly upon our experiences and sentiments. The frequent use in the old hymns of the words *Thou* and *Thy* are not a problem for me, since they often seem more appropriate for addressing God than the familiar word *You.* The use of *You* makes sense to use in public settings because we do not have formal and informal personal pronouns in modern English like that found in other languages. One collection I use is A. W. Tozer's *The Christian Book of Mystical Verse* (Harrisburg, Pa.: Christian Publications). Originally published in the early

1960s, it is still in print. Another is a volume of psalms, hymns, and spiritual songs I found in a secondhand book store and that features, among others, the verses of Isaac Watts.

Think about the character of God as you have discovered Him to be in your life so far. Experiment in particular with praising the qualities you have perceived by experience, in addition to the traits we traditionally affirm. Shape your praise like music, so that it has variety and expresses how you feel. You might find, as I do, that praying and worshiping out loud, when you are alone, is far more effective and satisfying than silent prayer. The emphasis here is on expressing your appreciation of God to God, recognizing that other activities are also appropriate during devotional times, such as petitionary prayers and intercession. However, these prayers will be driven by greater faith and confidence if you have cultivated an intimate awareness of God.

We should not expect every time of prayer or worship to keep generating the same response in us. Sometimes the presence of God in our hearts is a vibrant experience, touching the emotions. Other times we know His presence with our minds, much like we know the truth. Sometimes God seems ever so close to us. At other times He seems distant. There is variety in how He manifests Himself to us, just as there will be in how we express ourselves to Him.

7. *Connect your prayer and praise experiences to your workday environment.* If you tend to sense God's presence in churches or on retreats but not in the marketplace, use your imagination to picture Jesus beside you going through your day. It is a rather childlike method, but it can be effective. Eventually, instead of using pictures in your head, you will develop a consciousness of God's presence wherever you go because the Holy Spirit actually is wherever you go.

Observe all the physical objects about you from the tools of your trade to the structure of the building. Cultivate the realization that as each second goes by, God is holding together every molecule, every atom, every fragment of those objects. Were He to cease doing so any given microsecond, everything would disappear. As you visually review your familiar surroundings, thank God for the beauty of your world. If there is little beauty, thank Him for the practical value of its function.

Think about Jesus' attitude toward each person with whom you work. Reflect upon His hopes for their destiny. Develop an attitude toward them that is in harmony with what you might prayerfully perceive God wants to accomplish in their lives. Be aware that at any moment you may say words that will become important to someone, but you may never know when or to whom. Guard your tongue, so that whatever you say at work will be in harmony with what you utter in worship. Express appreciation for the contributions of others as though they are more valuable than your own. They may be.

8. *Be open to possible changes in the future.* The God with whom we live is consistent. He is going to use us primarily according to the gifts He has given us, but that does not necessarily mean in the same place forever. Some people are inclined to move toward change. Others like things to remain the same. In organizations, employees who like change enable development to take place, whereas the others provide stability. Both are valuable. When it comes to God's direction, however, do not let your natural inclinations prevent you from being sensitive to His timing for your life. That is why being able to hear God as an individual is so critical. God is an understanding ally when our natural inclinations might impede our progress toward a new goal or fresh opportunity.

PROTEST

There are those who would protest that much of what I have presented in support of distinctiveness merely encourages egotism, when everyone knows that Jesus calls us to humility. The verse usually quoted to represent this protest are the famous words of John the Baptist in John 3:30: "He must increase, but I must decrease" (KJV). It is assumed that this statement calls us to a relationship with God where we are to be so filled with His Spirit that we become decreasingly significant. The image given to illustrate what spirituality looks like portrays each of us like a vessel filled with our will, but which is gradually replaced with God's will. Following this logic, perfect spirituality would be to peer into the vessel and discover nothing of ourselves and everything of God. This sounds quite religious, but it flies in the face of the creative act of God who made man and approved what He made.

I am not recommending that we *pursue* distinctiveness. I am stating that we *are* distinctive by nature, which is to say by God's creative act. God didn't create us to become nothings. He created us to be the rulers of all things temporal and eventually take places of responsibility in the new kingdom. The problem with man usually is not that he thinks too much of himself. The difficulty is that he thinks too little of himself to believe what the Bible declares we are: princes and princesses of a new order. While man's sin often justifies the worst one can say about him, Christ's redemption requires that we confess the most happy ending there can possibly be in the story of man in his relationship with God.

The quote from John the Baptist has little to do with humility. The fact that John made the announcement indisputably displays his humility, but the content of the words announces the close of his ministry, given the arrival of the Messiah. Not only was his ministry to decrease but also the age it represented. The time of the church was soon going to begin, because its founder was laying the cornerstone. This Jesus through whom and for whom everything was made cannot be diminished by the vigor of our presence. After all, He invented our presence. He did not come to diminish us, but to raise us up as distinctive citizens of His new kingdom. We are not to be replaced by God's Spirit, but we are to be permeated by Him. The Holy Spirit is the only source of our distinctiveness, and we honor Him by being what He intends.

Where does this leave humility? Is it cast aside? How could it be when the Jesus we love displayed it? He did not do so by becoming a carpet for others to walk on. He did not hide His gifts. He recognized the reality of who He was and what He was called to do. Similarly, we know who we are. We are sinners, saved by grace. The fact of our sin should remove egotism and pretentiousness. The fact of grace supports our significance.

CHAPTER SIXTEEN

COMPETITION AND SECURITY

When I was a boy, I remember reading books by Charles Beebe, the naturalist who was known for descending into the sea in a steel bathysphere designed for deep sea observation. That was the beginning of my fascination with the innumerable varieties of life found in the earth's oceans.

One of my favorite creatures was, and still is, the sea turtle. While it isn't exotic, it is a well-designed, meek creature with interesting nesting habits. I am intrigued whenever I see film footage of hundreds of little sea turtles emerging from their sandy hatcheries above the surf of the ocean. However, I dread the inevitable scenes of gulls and other hungry birds raucously diving down to grab the helpless amphibians before they get to the safety of the water.

Hundreds upon hundreds of the little ones make a mad dash for the sea, but most never make it. Very few get into the ocean, and only a fraction of those reach maturity. For me that has always been a graphic reminder of what life is like under the curse of the Fall. It portrays what life has been like, not only for the animal kingdom, but also for human history. Humans make their mad dash for security only to have their lives snatched from them by accidents, wars, murders, disease, earthquakes, and floods, if they first escape with their lives from their mothers' wombs.

When physical survival has been achieved, there follows the effort to survive in the family, in school, and in the marketplace. People are competing everywhere for more money, more business, greater success, more fame, some ruthlessly running over associates to get ahead, a few actually planning the ruin of others.

Human survival on all levels has always been a dicey matter. How should the Christian think about all of this, especially since it is so much a part of the marketplace mentality where we often find ourselves? What should the Christian's attitude be toward the competitive drive within individuals and in corporations? Then, given the dynamics of a competitive secular culture, how does one feel secure as a Christian, surrounded by so much insecurity? These are not matters requiring one definitive conclusion, especially in respect to competition, because it is a dynamic subject, changing, in some respects, from decade to decade. I share my views with that in mind.

COMPETITION

Though there certainly are attitudes toward competition in Christian culture, there is no unified response to it in the church at large. Usually the political/economic setting of a particular congregation will determine its position, positive or negative. There have been a variety of reactions on the part of Christians, ranging from the formation of separatist communities, replacing the competitive interests of the marketplace with supportive systems, all the way to Christians in business competing with others in their fields of endeavor.

Many individuals take jobs that directly involve climbing ladders of success and then look for proof texts in their Bibles to justify their efforts. Or they simply conclude that since they are driven by their careers, they are not very spiritual. Others prefer to take jobs which keep them focused on work that has a perimeter that keeps them away from office politics and career competition. For still others, ministry organizations provide escape from the marketplace, but, as they soon discover, not always from career competition. Certainly, the idea of competition is closely associated with the concept of ambition. If as Christians we engage in it, it does seem somewhat suspect. If as Christians we avoid it, it does appear appropriately spiritual, but wimpy.

The traditional American understanding of competition is head-to-head challenge that makes one the winner and the other the loser.

However, that is not the full meaning of the word *compete*. The Latin contribution (*competere*) to the word refers to coming together, seeking together, or being suitable. We can easily see from such definitions how the Latin term is related to the English word *competent*, which suggests suitability related to work, or adequate ability. From there we go to the necessity of comparison, which leads to the selection of who is most suitable, and from there to rivalry for a position.

What I am suggesting is that the idea of coming together is of great importance, with rivalry creating the mechanism for doing so. Athletic events are useful examples in explaining this concept. When I was in high school, I loved to run. Coming together in rivalry with other runners intensified the quality of my performance. When rivals were there, I was a better runner. However, another factor, an artificial one, can be thrown into the situation. I represented my school. I did so just by attending it. I therefore could be perceived as running for my school. But representing a school has nothing to do with the joy of running. My school could be better or worse than the rival school, but it was not better or worse based on my running, though to hear my fellow students, it was.

If I gained the support of my fellow students, that was pleasing, but the support given me had more to do with healthy community attitudes than athletics. For example, in Britain and Europe soccer rivalries have actually ended with people being killed. That has everything to do with seriously unhealthy communities and nothing whatsoever to do with soccer. When cheers for a score mean jeers for a town, we are dealing with perniciousness. It turns competition into combat and destroys the pleasure of the game—and the game really is the point. Because our society often uses athletics for purposes that have nothing to do with athletic performance, it thereby corrupts our understanding of what competition is supposed to be. As Christians, we should display a redemptive view.

Let us now look at competition in the context of our professions: careers in the marketplace. When we engage in professional competition it increases quality and performance. Surgeons who specialize on the heart do better when there are other heart surgeons around. When a surgeon engages in such professional rivalry, it is stimulating and good for everyone. But when surgeons convert professional competition into personal rivalry out of jealousy or greed, they open their souls to contempt. In professional rivalry the "win" works for the client. In personal rivalry, the focus is upon the devaluation or the elimination of the opponent. There is no win.

In business, competition works in favor of the consumer, because a rival business wins by providing the most favorable terms to the client. Rival businesses are healthy for each other, because competition keeps them on their toes. Now if a rival uses unfair practices, it may make it impossible for the competition to stay in business. That destroys the natural rivalry, and in the absence of competition quality will be reduced, which is not in favor of the client or consumer. So, referring back to athletics, what we want is not a game that eliminates, but a game that stimulates. That kind of setting is the most productive setting, and that is the kind of competition Christian business people ought to support and sustain.

Competition never means the destruction of the rival. Winning has no relationship to destruction whatsoever. Wanting to win creates the opportunities. That is why the apostle Paul could use his metaphors about running races and winning crowns. He was intensely competitive, thereby causing growth in the church and in countless individuals. But I believe those competitive gifts were peculiar to the apostle Paul. That is how God made him, and so they are not a model for others. Timothy, for example, did not display competitive behavior, nor did Jesus Christ, for that matter. The conclusion I would make, then, is that God has made some people competitive and others not. We should be aware of who we are in this regard. Assuming a competitive role without the supporting gifts is exhausting and will prove nothing of value. The exercise of competitive gifts needs to be tempered by the Holy Spirit, and not by any other compulsive force or reason.

SECURITY

One reason many people are running on a competitive treadmill that does not fit them is because they are driven by fear concerning their security. I can understand this. Whether we look at the big picture of humanity or the events of individual lives, we are convinced that life is precarious. No wonder we look for a place of safety. No wonder so many people do not venture forth in life. It can be dangerous.

So while my temperament and values reject the idea of paying for security by accepting years of misfit work or placement in a safe but inappropriate career, I understand why people do it. The long-ing for a haven of safety makes a lot of sense. Isn't that what Jesus responded to when He called people to come to Him if they were weary and burdened so He could give them rest? Isn't it the same understanding that caused Him to use the humble metaphor of the mother hen?

> O Jerusalem, Jerusalem, the city that murders the prophets and stones the messengers sent to her! How often have I longed to gather your children, as a hen gathers her brood under her wings; but you would not let me. (Matthew 23:37 NEB)

Old Testament theology about our security is most strongly portrayed in Psalm 91. Safety is promised to those who trust God in the face of raging tempests, pestilence, arrows, serpents, and other dangers of all kinds. This promise is based on the simple rubric of rewarding the righteous, which is the consistent theme of Old Testament Scriptures.

The evidence for Israel's belief in God was objective. There was something to see as a result of your action. You do right, and God treats you right. You do wrong, and everything goes wrong: you lose battles, your crops wither, disease infects you. One would think that that would have encouraged contagious righteousness in Israel. No, their hearts were predictably fickle. They were too flawed to regain paradise.

The New Testament portrays our relationship with God some-what differently. The relationship remains one based upon God's concern for His people, but it is also one where Jesus calls us to take up our cross and follow Him. Christians are peculiarly de-scribed as sheep being led to the slaughter. As we know from histo-ry, being a Christian can bring persecution or even martyrdom, but whatever happens, being a Christian also means that we cannot be separated from God's faithful love.

This is not quite like the black-and-white assurance of Psalm 91. But in actuality, something greater is going on. The New Testa-ment saints are more than people who follow God. They (and we) are daughters and sons of God. We possess the security character-ized by membership in an intimate family. We can rely on the faith-ful oversight of a spiritual Father.

How do we know we are not suffering delusions about our relationship with God? Because His Holy Spirit, who dwells within us, is an ever-present witness supporting the truth of our permanent connection to God.

How do we know we can undertake a difficult task we know God has called us to do? Because God directly supplies the wherewithal through the empowering of the Holy Spirit. In the context of Christianity, the courage to achieve our ambitions and to take venturesome steps of faith is based on the security of God's call and the power of His Spirit in all the roles we play in our lives.

The Holy Spirit provides understanding. That is how the disciples could be so sure that when they followed Jesus they were not following an illusion.

> Jesus asked his disciples, 'Who do men say the Son of Man is?' They answered, 'Some say John the Baptist, others Elijah, others Jeremiah, or one of the prophets.' 'And you,' he asked, 'who do you say I am?' Simon Peter answered: 'You are the Messiah, the Son of the living God.' Then Jesus said: 'Simon son of Jonah, you are favoured indeed! You did not learn that from mortal man; it was revealed to you by my heavenly Father.' (Matthew 16:13–18 NEB)

What was a revelatory experience for the apostle Peter is repeated for us who live in the age of the church and who have not seen the physical Jesus Christ. Our obstinate belief in the reality of Jesus is due to continuing revelation of the Holy Spirit within us as individuals.

> For ye have not received the spirit of bondage again to fear; but ye have received the Spirit of adoption, whereby we cry Abba, Father. The Spirit itself beareth witness with our spirit, that we are the children of God: and if children, then heirs; heirs of God, and joint-heirs with Christ. (Romans 8:15–17 KJV)

Our security as Christians cannot rest in the church we attend. Our security cannot be gained by making a ritual artifact of the Bible. Nor can it be derived from a commitment to doctrinal purity, or from moral living, or from a spiritual mentor. Our security in Christ is established by God. He is the initiator, the One who made the first move toward us, and He does it personally.

He does it by the power of the Holy Spirit in us, person to person. We did not become Christians because we were smart enough to pray the sinner's prayer, or because we realized our guilt and did something about it, or because we were clever enough to respond to the Gospel when it was preached. Those activities only became meaningful in our lives when God inhabited them. He comes first.

All the activities on our part—praying, repenting, listening to the Gospel, being converted, and reading the Bible—are empty religious rites without the presence of the Holy Spirit, who gives us power to come into the kingdom of righteousness. Mankind is prone to religion, be it pagan, scientific, philosophical, economic, or Christian. God simply is not interested in nugatory religious actions even when they include activities that He Himself established. That was true in Old Testament days, and it is true now. Imagine the shock of Isaiah's message to Judah when he brings to them words such as these:

> Your countless sacrifices, what are they to me?
>   says the Lord.
> I am sated with whole-offerings of rams
>   and the fat of buffaloes;
> I have no desire for the blood of bulls,
>   of sheep and of he-goats. . . .
> Who asked you for this? . . .
>   The offer of your gifts is useless,
> the reek of sacrifice is abhorrent to me.
>   (Isaiah 1:11–13 NEB)

I suspect that the hearers of these scathing words were not inclined to remind God that He Himself had established the system of sacrifices and offerings. They were forced to realize the difference between what God intended and what had degenerated into empty religious observance. Even their prayers were condemned!

> When you lift your hands outspread in prayer,
> I will hide my eyes from you.
> Though you offer countless prayers,
>   I will not listen.
>   (Isaiah 1:15 NEB)

It is easy for modern Christians to see the folly of vain religious rites in the Old Testament because those rites are unfamiliar to us. Our difficulty is to see at what point Christian rituals and programs become meaningless because they are so familiar. They have all kinds of nice sentiments attached to them. But they cannot contain genuine vitality when they are not inspired and inhabited by the presence of the Holy Spirit.

The day anyone becomes a Christian is the first day of a life-time of temptation to convert spiritual expression into religious labor. The New Testament records of Jesus' reaction to the priests of His day are often shocking. He knew that they were vile men carrying out with great precision every detail of every rite of God's law.

> Alas for you, lawyers and Pharisees, hypocrites! You pay tithes of mint and dill and cummin; but you have overlooked the weightier demands of the Law, justice, mercy, and good faith. It is these you should have practiced, without neglecting the others. Blind guides! You strain off a midge yet gulp down a camel! . . .

> Alas for you lawyers and Pharisees, hypocrites! You are like tombs covered with whitewash; they look well from outside, but inside they are full of dead men's bones and all kinds of filth. So it is with you: outside you look like honest men, but inside you are brim-full of hypocrisy and crime. (Matthew 23:23–24; 27–28 NEB)

As we proceed with these thoughts, we do not want to lose sight of our objective: to understand our security in the stewardship of our lives. What should begin to emerge is the realization that our ambitions can be as empty as Judah's sacrifices or as meaningless as any unspiritual religious activity.

Looking at appearances, it would have been hard to differentiate genuine Old Testament sacrifices from those that were abhorrent to God. The priests had to go through the same procedures either way. Similarly, it can be difficult to identify legitimate expressions of our ambitions from those which are not. Remember that God looks on the heart. Someone may be gifted to be in the spotlight and in that position achieve worthwhile and satisfying results. For another, what looks like a similar performance may in reality be a grossly egocentric event. The difference between the two depends upon the quality and the object of their ambitions. For whom, ultimately, are they performing? Either we work under the guidance of the Holy Spirit or not; we desire to please God or not. Authentic achievements cannot take place without God's participation in whatever we do. For that we are totally dependent upon the grace of the Holy Spirit's presence in us.

It is critical that we live lives filled with the Spirit. Instead of a plan, we then have a guide. Instead of desperately grasping at any opportunity, we have direction. Instead of being intimidated by all the forces—economic, political, and social—that sweep over and around us, we have confidence. Instead of emotional insecurity, we have peace that passes all understanding. What usually is blocking the flow of the Holy Spirit is failure to be obedient regarding the step upon which we are now standing. While we cast about to determine what is the matter with us, we ignore that which is at our feet.

Considering how many people there are in the world with whom God is relating, many find it difficult to believe that He can relate intimately with each person. How can God empower and relate to so many people at one time? In asking this question we impute human characteristics to God. Human relationships are a matter of how much energy an individual has to invest in another and whether energy is returned. That is why unrequited love exhausts. We cannot measure how much energy God puts in His love toward any one of us because He does not act out of energy but out of power. Energy fluctuates even when the term is used to describe our emotions and feelings. God's power is His state of sovereignty, out of which He is capable of engaging an unlimited number of people in relationships.

God does not spend power. His power involves no variance in degree, though it appears in different modes of expression. For example, we can refer to His power of judgment, or the power of His mercy, or the power of His grace. The observable titanic power of God holding the entire universe in existence, with no let-up since its beginning, should make it easy for us to understand the constancy of His love toward any one of us. We are utterly secure in His power. Therefore our future is secure.

It is secure even as we go through death. The Holy Spirit does not abandon ship when death comes knocking on our door. Death is not stronger than the source of life. We go through that door with the Holy Spirit, who has been always with us and is still present with us, flooding our consciousness with His love as we go home to a life more brilliant than we can now conceive.

A CAUTION

It has been fashionable from time to time for some people to refer to the reality of the spiritual realm but equating the Spirit of Christianity with the spirits of other religions, or with Native American ceremonies, as if they were all foundationally related in some way. However, when the Bible refers to the Spirit, it means the Holy Spirit, who is not an it but a person. We refer to Him with the personal pronoun *He.*

The Holy Spirit is not an amorphous spook, wraith, or specter. He does not work by magic or operate as if He were not a distinct person of the Trinity. The Christian is not someone who comes under the good influence of *a* spirit. The Christian is one who has a particular relationship with a person called Jesus Christ through *the* Holy Spirit, who is sent by the Father. He is the creative expression of the Godhead. He sustains the universe and empowers people.

Without Him there is nothing. With Him there is energy, inspiration, motivation, an intensity of love, and overwhelming vitality. With Him we can come to an understanding of the remarkable love Jesus has for us. There is a deep chasm between the eternal kingdom of God and the condition in which we find ourselves, between God and the sinner. The cross of Jesus bridges that chasm.

When we hear of that bridge, we suspect that it most likely is an illusion. It is too happy an ending to the story to be real. But the Holy Spirit convinces us that the bridge indeed is real. He is the source of that knowledge. More than that, He enables us to cross over on it. Once we have come into a relationship with Jesus, we can live our lives and go through our deaths with ultimate confidence that we are in His capable care and love. He knows the way, since He has already walked it. He sends His Holy Spirit to assure and empower us while we are on our journey. We are ultimately secure in Him.